'For too long, policy makers of all stripes have 1
an industrial process than can be made more effi
standardization, keener competition, and the unlea
The story of Hampstead School illustrates vividl
of educational achievement, and it couldn't be m
that education is not an industrial process but a human one that has
to be hand crafted to individual talents and circumstances. It is about
students, teachers, parents, and communities learning together. This
story is a powerful testament to the messy nuances, daily challenges, and
heartfelt triumphs of real education in the real world of human struggle
and achievement. It is a story of diversity, creativity, collaboration, and
innovation. It is, above all, a story of the power of humane, sensitive and
visionary leadership. It is a story that is played out every day in great
schools everywhere, each in its own way. It is the real story of education
and it has to be told and retold until it is properly understood by anyone
who claims to have a genuine interest in what education is and what it
really involves.'

Professor Emeritus Sir Ken Robinson, University of Warwick

'I have always considered myself extremely lucky to have attended
Hampstead School, a fact hard to explain to the sort of people whose
interest in a school begins and ends with its league tables. To me, it was an
exemplary inner city state school for reasons that sometimes included those
league tables but more often stretched far beyond them. It was more than
an education; it was an experience – one of the most fulfilling of my life.
It's a pleasure to be able to hear so many former students expressing the
complexity of that experience; what it meant to them to be in a school that
believed everyone deserved at least the same opportunity – whatever their
ability, class or race – and for free. It was by instilling this belief in their
students that the school hoped to give us the sense that we were nothing
if not pure potential. Of course, not everyone took up the opportunities
offered. But many did, far more than seem possible or likely. (I was one of
the unlikely ones.) This book, initiated by our headteacher, explains how
it was done, and how something similar might be achieved elsewhere. It's
essential reading for anyone who cares about state education, both its past
and – more vitally – its future.'

Zadie Smith

'In these barren days of educational policy and politics, it is wonderful to feel the heat of a real red-blooded school; a successful school running on care and creativity; a school that didn't always get it right, but was loved by the vast majority of those who worked and learned there – even those who were trouble at the time.'

Professor Guy Claxton, Professor of the Learning Sciences, University of Winchester

'This deeply moving text interweaves voices of former students of Hampstead School with those of governors, parents, teachers, and leaders over a period of almost 45 years. Revealing the complex, lived experiences of a vibrant comprehensive school community, it conveys powerfully, through first-hand accounts, the lifelong legacies of this community of diversity and humanity.

The fruits of recognition, relationship, and respect permeate these raw-data narratives, together with a commitment to creativity, innovation, and trust, equality and diversity, reflection and lifelong learning. This rich testimony offers rare depth of insight into the too-often invisible aspects of high aspiration: the attention to detail that is born of leadership that is demanding, distributed, and democratic, and which seeks to model lifelong learning.

This extraordinary text conveys the far-reaching effects of professionals who care. As English education policy moves toward narrower definitions of school success, through "core knowledge", the accounts in this unique book provide inspiration for those who seek to understand how rich and extended provision changes lives. They show us compellingly how intricate, extensive, and necessary such provision is.'

Professor Anna Craft, University of Exeter and the Open University

'In America, education reform is described as "the civil rights struggle of our time". Reformers are building new schools and emphasising the need for transformational leadership. As with so many other cultural phenomena this zeal is rapidly crossing the Atlantic. And with good reason. Today in the UK children from the poorest families, who are eligible for free school meals, are only half as likely to get five A*–C grades at GCSE as their wealthier peers.

In our urgency to address this injustice we would do well to remember (as one of those US education reformers, Wendy Kopp, is fond of saying) that in education there are no 'silver bullets'.

Instead, successful new schools are doing what schools like Hampstead School, under the leadership of Tamsyn Imison, have long known to be "what works".

In this wonderfully well-deserved homage to a remarkable school, one teacher writes about the need to banish cynicism and complacency with a "no excuses" and "success for all" culture. She describes teaching *Paradise Lost* to an A level class, 12 of whom were accepted at Oxford or Cambridge in one year. Another writes about the orchestras and performances that students from all backgrounds participated in. In all of these testimonies the school's focus on "relationships" is overwhelmingly evident.

Although the book covers Hampstead School over a 20-year period from 1980, none of these ideas has become outdated, nor are they unsuited to the more recent challenges education faces. The book serves as a timely reminder that what works in education is seldom revolutionary. We all know most of it: things like great leadership, high standards, no selection, no excuses, and rich extra-curricular opportunities.

What *is* revolutionary is a commitment to ensure that all students will succeed. One teacher writes, "As the attainment gap between rich and poor widens ... I see I was fortunate to experience at an early stage in my career how comprehensive education and commitment to inclusion can achieve both excellence and equity."

This is a book that gives the reader that same vicarious experience, and as such it's an invaluable contribution to the cause of educational reform in this country.'

Lord Puttnam

'This book is, in its own words, a collection of glimpses into what a school can be – not just any old school but a true non-selective urban comprehensive with students from every kind of background and from all over the world. Many contributors – students, teachers, other staff, governors, others too – bring the school alive.

"You have to be lost to be found and this is what I was", writes a student who arrived as a refugee from the Balkans. Every contribution illustrates that all our geese can be swans. It's a tale that lifts the spirits.'

Sir Geoffrey Holland, former Permanent Secretary at the Department for Education and Skills, and Chair of the former Learning and Skills Development Agency

'For most of the period covered by this book, I have observed at first hand many of the developments it describes.

I have known Hampstead School since the 1980s and have always seen it as a part of the answer to those who dismiss comprehensive schools. It has demonstrated over many years that a school that celebrates diversity and creativity can also encourage learning and achievement. The book itself serves both as testimony to what one particular school has achieved and advocacy of the potential of comprehensive education more generally. The accounts from pupils, parents, teachers and governors are really inspiring and give the reader an authentic feel of how a truly inclusive school can succeed.

The book demonstrates how leadership at all levels, from the governors and head teacher through to the school council, is crucial to building shared values, securing engagement and commitment from all stakeholders, and celebrating achievements of all kinds. The external contributors to the book also show how shortsighted it is to discount the role of local authorities and universities in building the sort of professional culture that fosters school improvement and individual achievement.'

Professor Geoff Whitty, Director Emeritus, Institute of Education, University of London, and Professor of Management, University of Bath

'*Comprehensive Achievements* inspires educationalists to be more creative in their approach to the curriculum at a time when schools are in the main overly directed. It describes a school where success is to be celebrated, confidence is built by developing the trust and imagination of students and staff, all of whom are encouraged to work collaboratively towards their shared values, culminating in a dynamic, aspirational community of "lead learners". Something that is as relevant today as when it was introduced.'

Terri Broughton, Vice Principal (Teaching and Learning) King's Lynn Academy

Comprehensive Achievements

This book is dedicated to all past, present, and future students, teachers and associate staff, parents and governors, and their local authority and higher education partners in non-selective schools in England and elsewhere

Comprehensive Achievements

All our geese are swans

Edited by Tamsyn Imison, Liz Williams, and Ruth Heilbronn

A Trentham Book
Institute of Education Press

First published in 2014 by the Institute of Education, University of London, 20 Bedford Way, London WC1H 0AL

www.ioe.ac.uk/ioepress

British Library Cataloguing-in-Publication Data:
A catalogue record for this book is available from the British Library

ISBNs
978-1-85856-530-9 (paperback)
978-1-85856-546-0 (PDF eBook)
978-1-85856-547-7 (ePub eBook)
978-1-85856-548-4 (Kindle eBook)

Typeset by Quadrant Infotech (India) Pvt Ltd
Printed by CPI Group (UK) Ltd, Croydon, CR0 4YY

Cover image: Theo Games Petrohilos, www.theogamespetrohilos.com

Contents

Acknowledgements

The editors would like to thank Rene Branton-Saran, a governor of Hampstead School from the early 1970s to 2000, for her significant support of this book. It would not have been written or published without her.

About the editors

Dame Tamsyn Imison is currently an education strategist and was formerly head teacher of Hampstead School from 1984 to 2000. She was a member of the Secondary Heads Association (SHA) council, and executive and chair of the SHA Information and Communications Technology and Equal Opportunities committees from 1994 to 1999. She is a member of the National Advisory Committee on Creative and Cultural Education. She was vice-chair of the National Judging Panel Teaching Awards in 2000–4, chair of the University of London careers board from 1997 to 2003, and an appraiser for the Girls' Day School Trust and various local education authorities. Her presentations and published work include the subjects of leadership, ICT, creativity, schools of the future, post-16 education, and women leaders. She was a consultant for SHA, the London Leadership Centre and Cornwall College. She is a trustee of Eastfeast (artists and horticulturalists working with children and teachers in schools), the Lifelong Learning Foundation, and the Society for the Furtherance of Critical Philosophy. Tamsyn is a patron of the Campaign for Learning and 5x5x5=creativity (artists and cultural centres working with children and teachers in schools).

Liz Williams was a governor of Hampstead School for 17 years, nine of them as chair while Tamsyn Imison was head. During her career she has been involved in a range of full-time and freelance publishing activities, starting with *Nature*, the science journal. In the mid-1970s in Doha she produced and presented a regular science programme for the Qatar Broadcasting Service. After providing voluntary support for two parent campaigning groups in the 1980s, she worked for 20 years at the Advisory Centre for Education. She is currently a trustee of Research and Information on State Education (RISE).

Ruth Heilbronn is a lecturer in education at the Institute of Education, University of London. She is a specialist in teacher education, the philosophy of education, and languages in education. Responsibilities have included leading the teacher education special interest group and being subject leader for the PGCE modern foreign languages (MFL), team leader for PGCE professional studies, and module leader for the Master's of teaching. Research, publishing, and consultancy include the induction of newly qualified teachers, mentoring for the growth of professional knowledge and understanding, and the use of professional development portfolios in professional learning. She has wide experience of senior management in urban secondary schools, including responsibility for continuing professional development (CPD), and has led various MFL teams as a head of department and LEA adviser. She is an experienced editor and author, and an executive member of the Philosophy of Education Society of Great Britain.

Preface

Sir Tim Brighouse

This is the 'story of a school': or perhaps more accurately, the frequent shaking of a kaleidoscope, with each image providing a beautiful glimpse of a school's life. In the period that the story covers – 1980 to 2000 – Hampstead was an extraordinary school, and one that commanded huge respect in both its own and the wider community. So the glimpses of what a school can be like are especially vivid and compelling.

The editors have chosen to pick out three themes in their introduction: diversity, learning, and creativity. In respect of the last of these, as well as in its entirety, the book brings to mind a much earlier *Story of a School* – a ministry pamphlet published in 1949 and reprinted in the mid-1950s as advice to primary schools. It was written by a head teacher about his approach to curriculum and school organization, with a foreword from the minister of education encouraging schools to do likewise, and try out new methods based on their professional judgement. Such an approach by a secretary of state seems surreal now.

This book straddles the period that starts when the general consensus about educational good still held sway, and when the secretary of state was content to have just three powers, but ends when he had almost 2,000. So it commences when schools were expected to think 'curriculum', and finishes when the curriculum had been nationalized and was therefore provided, and when the first tentative steps had been taken to tell teachers how and what to teach. For Hampstead that was only part of the change. The Inner London Education Authority (ILEA) was abolished and Hampstead became part of Camden. Teacher industrial action in the mid-1980s destroyed many schools, but not Hampstead. And the introduction of the General Certificate of Secondary Education (GCSE) to replace the old General Certificate of Education (GCE) and Certificate of Secondary Education (CSE) was another diversion it took in its stride. Its authors confess that one of their purposes in writing the book is to strike a blow against perceptions of the 'bog standard comprehensive school'. The stories the contributors tell make an incontrovertible case that there was nothing 'bog standard' about Hampstead, although it was, of course, comprehensive. In addition, however, it shows how it is possible for a well-led school with well-chosen staff to hold strong to their professional and moral beliefs, and in doing so resonate with their pupils, parents, and the wider school community.

As the editors argue, it is possible to make sense of the whole through the map of diversity, learning, and creativity, and I wouldn't disagree with that. Rather I would like to offer a matrix of four other elements that each illuminate those themes: specialness, staff development, student involvement, and leadership. They are all features of outstanding schools like Hampstead, which this volume so graphically illuminates.

Of these, perhaps the most important is specialness. It was once remarked that unless a child has a worthwhile relationship with at least one member of staff in a school, they aren't really at school. They may be physically present, but they aren't there in spirit. In my understanding, you increase the likelihood of that happening if you can discover what might be called the 'Kes' factor of each and every one of the pupils in a school. It is called the Kes factor after the 1950s, never-to-be-forgotten book and film of that name, which evocatively describes the travails of the youngster for whom life, including school, meant very little beyond his pet kestrel, and whose love and affinity for the kestrel proved a bulwark against a surfeit of humiliation and mockery. Hampstead was a school that saw it as part of its business to discover the Kes interests of their pupils, and to worry when a pupil appeared to have none. Hampstead staff did more than worry: they would seek to introduce and share enthusiasms that might incubate a Kes factor in a pupil's life. For the Kes factor would be a key to a love of learning, of a lifelong fulfilling interest to energize them, to the delight of themselves and those they would meet. The staff at Hampstead, it seems, were selected for their own Kes factors. They too were all special and treated as such, so that in turn they created the events and activities that inspired so many pupils. It was a school full of Kes interests, and the chances of pupils being invisible, demotivated, or at risk were therefore much reduced.

Schools like Hampstead make the case for this 'specialness' factor that is overlooked in the much ploughed field of 'school improvement'. It is worth reflecting too that in 1980, when this book's story starts, 'school improvement' had not really been invented. Until Michael Rutter's *Fifteen Thousand Hours: Secondary schools and their effects on children* (1979), researchers didn't think schools made a difference. From the beginning, however, and perhaps in part inspired by Rutter's findings, Hampstead's head and all her staff, together with the whole school community, acted with the certainty that what they did made a huge difference. The school itself was special.

The second factor of staff development shines through this book: the editors specifically refer to it, and every staff contribution is supportive testimony. Staff at Hampstead seem to enjoy four key conditions of service. Once they have been selected, they enjoy responsibility and permitting circumstances, and are given new experiences and respect. Responsibility means they are trusted to lead some aspect of school life, while permitting circumstances means they operate in a culture where people are encouraged to try out new ideas and take risks, and know that they won't be blamed if things go wrong. New experiences involves meeting new challenges in your career development and, importantly, knowing you will be given support when you take them. Respect needs no explanation. Unless teachers are respected, they won't stay long. It is a sad commentary on politicians and system leaders that nowadays real respect for teachers appears to be entirely down to the school. But the Hampstead story here provides a wealth of testimony about how teachers there knew they were respected. As such, it provides a timely reminder to present school leaders, harassed as they are by ever fiercer accountability with ever narrower measures, that there are ways to value and grow staff.

So staff development, whether manifested in the 90 per cent who were involved in more formal further learning, or in the jobs they were entrusted to do as new to them, was key to its success.

So too was student involvement. It was pretty unusual at that time to have the sort of vibrantly active school council to which these pages testify. As such, it is a forerunner to the closely analysed student involvement being encouraged now in those schools at the leading edge of practice. Like Hampstead, these schools know it isn't simply about practising democratic vehicles, but about involving students in the many management tasks of the school, in co-constructing the curriculum, in assessing and assisting with learning, in not just being taught but providing a model of thinking for themselves and acting for others. That is exactly what Hampstead student witnesses testify to here.

Finally, running like a live wire through it all is leadership. All the witnesses show how they were given opportunities to lead, and of course in many cases their subsequent careers bear witness to how well they took them. Before shared or distributed leadership was endlessly talked about in leadership and management courses and through the National College for School Leadership, Hampstead was doing it. The school was led by a team of people who knew that their five vital tasks were to create energy, grow capacity, create an environment fit for learning, extend the school's vision, and chart improvement. If you want to know what is meant by each of the five, hold them in your mind as a map as you read this book.

The school leadership team knew each other well enough to know who was good at what, and that they were part of a great enterprise where each helped the other. So they tried to remember people's birthdays and be solicitous at times of difficulty. They took the blame for others' failure when commitment and effort were not in question, and were generous with praise for jobs well done. Like all 'good enough' teachers and leaders, they tried to model behaviour and hoped it would be infectious. So they were liberal with acts of unexpected kindness. For example, the head would loan out her Suffolk cottage/retreat for weekends to members of staff for staff development or just a well-needed rest.

In modelling her own behaviour, the head exuded optimism – sometimes when she knew optimism to be scarcely justified, but believing that futures are shaped by one's own attitudes. She minimized crisis and regarded complexity as fun. She had a bottomless well of intellectual curiosity and a complete absence of self-pity. She knew that she and her colleagues were like actor-managers in provincial theatres. Once it was decided what the play would be, the actors would learn their parts, and the show would be put on as no other production had been put on before. The witnesses here show just how good the shows were. Yet the image I have chosen is flawed. It was perhaps more like jazz improvisation on many occasions, where all knew the need to play from the same score, but allowed sufficient individual expression to keep them alive and perpetually interested and interesting.

The head and her colleagues at Hampstead during the 20 years chronicled here exemplify a quote from George Bernard Shaw's *Man and Superman,* where his character describes what he calls the 'true joy in life'. He wants

> ... to be thoroughly used up when I die. The more I work, the more
> I live. Life is no brief candle to me, it's a sort of splendid torch and
> I have got hold of it for the moment and I want to make it burn
> as brightly as possible before handing it on to future generations.

Well, that's what a great school does. Read on and you will see what it means. The final section provides the context. There and in the preceding chapters you will find entries beautifully written, and which, taken together, provide an unvarnished description of how urban schools really are, and why we should renew our support for them, by sending our children and our children's children there and supporting them in any way we can.

Chapter 1

Introduction

Tamsyn Imison, Liz Williams, and Ruth Heilbronn

Background

This book is published at a time when schools in England are radically changing their organization and governance, rejecting a founding principle of the 1944 Education Act of education as a public service, and the ideal of 'the common school' (Dewey, 1916), in which an aim of education is to nurture a sense of community. We write to capture what a comprehensive school did and could do when conditions were favourable, and we offer this portrait of a successful, thriving comprehensive – Hampstead School – between the years 1980 and 2000 to express and endorse the foundational principles that should underpin all schools. We challenge the idea that comprehensive education leads to dull, uninspired teaching, as suggested by the term 'bog-standard comprehensive'. There is no such thing as a 'standard' school either. All schools have their own ethos, formed by the leadership, management, students, parents, outside involvement, and many other factors. The book illustrates how education could be broad-based and holistic as well as vibrant and creative, and could enable children to love learning and develop as rounded people, in addition to passing examinations.

The book is an initiative of the former head teacher, Tamsyn Imison, who asked contributors to write about how they came to the school, their experiences and achievements, and how they have since moved on. The resulting 50-plus voices are organized alphabetically in sections, with students, parents, staff – many of whom were also parents of students there – and governors. These voices are contextualized by the testimony and history of the local education authorities and higher education partners. The voices richly illustrate what is known from the literature on leadership: that the head teacher has a seminal role to play in developing an educational vision and enabling its achievement (Earley and Weindling, 2004; Leithwood and Riehl, 2003). But a significant additional factor is the power of devolved leadership, not just to staff but students as well. This demonstrates that the school had become 'a learning community' (Stoll *et al.*, 2006), as well as a community of learners, and reinforces what is known from the literature: that learning is a social activity (Watkins, 2005 and 2010).

More than 20 education acts were passed during the years covered by this book: a number of events are mentioned by contributors for the impact they had on the school. Among these are the 1987 Teachers' Pay and Conditions Act that ended teachers' industrial action, and the key 1988 Education Reform Act, brought in by Kenneth Baker, which introduced the national curriculum and Local Management of Schools (LMS), where schools gained direct control of their budgets. The 1988 Act also paved the way for the abolition of the Inner London Education Authority in 1990 (see Peter Newsam's overview of the ILEA and Hampstead School in Chapter 5). Peter Mitchell's account of setting up the Camden Local Education shows how the effects of the ILEA abolition were mitigated by various means, including the appointment of a strong team of inspectors. The 1991 Parents' Charter is also significant in promising published examination results. This led to performance tables, arguably the beginnings of teaching to the test, and linked to Ofsted's establishment in 1992 (with Chris Woodhead as its first chief inspector). At the end of the period covered by the book, Tony Blair's premiership, with David Blunkett as education secretary, ushered in a more supportive regime, with Mike Tomlinson becoming chief inspector in 2000 (Gillard, 2011).

Within this context the accounts in this book testify to the school's achievements. Among other factors three themes emerge strongly: the celebration of diversity and the strong emphasis on learning and creativity.

Diversity

Social and ethnic diversity is valued by students and staff at Hampstead School. Students value making friends 'across a wide range of backgrounds' (David Sunderland); 'the opportunity to be educated within my home area among a broad spectrum of people' (Megan Smith); 'all kinds of people, all hanging out together, day in, day out for years, all part of this same thing, undeniable' (Lilah Holywell); with 'very few problems of racism or bullying … down to the ethos of the school and how the school is united' (Robbie Ferguson). Parents and teachers shared this view and many teachers sent their children to Hampstead, an indication of confidence in the school. Andrea Berkeley indicates how this ultimately impacts on the wider society:

> I observe that this social ease with my daughters, the ability to mix and communicate with people from different backgrounds, is indeed the result of social change. But the contribution of

comprehensive education to this very social change is rarely recognized.

The school's stress on the value of all individuals, and its insistence that all should succeed, encouraged students to flourish:

> When I think back to being the only boy in the school dance troupe, giving a class presentation on the artistry of Darcey Bussell, and asking for a CD of Puccini arias as a prize for winning a science quiz, I simply don't know how I ever escaped having the crap kicked out of me ... In this environment, 'difference' was normalized.
>
> (Magid El-Bushra)

This normalization of individuality was critical for some:

> My three years at Hampstead were transformative. I learnt how to be human, not 'disabled'. I made enduring, deep friendships that remain. I had more fun than I had ever had, including acting in a fabulous production of *Joseph and the Amazing Technicolor Dreamcoat*, and I was never, ever bullied ... I don't think that this could have happened except in a comprehensive.
>
> (David Ruebain)

Yet the diversity had its challenges. As Magid El-Bushra went on to remark: 'Let's not kid ourselves, Hampstead was rough. As Ms Daulphin used to say, "Some of the students go to Oxbridge, and some go to prison".' In response to this challenge:

> Effective personalization was essential for teaching to be engaging and enjoyable ... for students to make good progress. In turn, this signalled the importance of continuously developing staff and maintaining a sharp focus on improving pedagogy, both at departmental and whole-school level.
>
> (Olly Button)

Respect for the individuality of teachers and students in this diverse setting required trust, for example through the school council, valued by students and staff alike. As Robbie Ferguson said in his *Your Shout* on Carlton TV, 'Having a school council makes us feel like we have a voice in the running of our school, giving us control over our school lives'. Staff views are voiced by Mark Mayne, among others, that 'the culture of the school was deeply responsive to [the] student voice ... Here was a group of students from across the years, discussing issues through shared procedures while maintaining a sense of hierarchy and respect', and George Reynoldson comments favourably that 'the pupils set the rules so they did not break them'.

Trust in a diverse staff, with individual approaches to curricula and initiatives was also apparent, and the senior team showed preparedness to take risks. For example, Mark Everett reports:

> I was lucky enough to be given the opportunity to run a science week. Never having been able to do things in small measures, this whole-school event rivalled the many other designated weeks that the senior team was brave enough to entrust to young teachers.
>
> (Mark Everett)

Above all, Hampstead was responsive to a changing school community, as seen from the arrival of a significant number of unaccompanied refugee children. Students testify to the support that was given. 'It was perfect, aimed and tender ... Shoulder to cry on, mother to hug, father to keep safe, friend in need' (Ediba-Bakira Trbonja-Kapic).

The accounts from Athy Demetriades, Soren Jensen, and Joanna de Regibus give striking background to the support and development that was offered, and the contribution of Glen Stevens indicates how necessary such work still is and how conditions have not changed for many of the school students.

Learning for all

The school credo, *Learning Together, Achieving Together,* was clearly more than a rhetorical device. Judging from strong evidence of collaborative learning in many of the student contributions and the belief in 'an environment in which students could learn' (Angella Hodgson), it was a way of life. The diversity outlined in the previous section is seen as a positive contribution to learning, and many students comment in one way or another that the social and cultural mix of the school was part of their learning to live in the adult world in the widest sense, beyond achieving qualifications. It is also apparent that this was felt as a privilege.

Achieving Together can be evidenced by the range and success in examination results, and:

> The clear message came through that *all* young people can achieve good things, and success goes much wider than academic achievement. It was a good step forward when results from

vocational qualifications were reported alongside GCSEs in national tables.

(Liz Williams)

Learning Together suggests a community of practice that develops and shares its expertise. This was undoubtedly a strong part of the school culture. For example, John Carruthers's contribution evidences and contextualizes his own learning as a student, the support he was given to achieve, and how he then became a lynchpin for staff development in the early days of IT literacy for all. Another former student, Megan Smith, attests to the learning achieved through 'not just curriculum learning, but learning through a wealth of other activities', which is highlighted in the next section on creativity. There were nested contexts that formed this collegiate learning community, starting from the commitment of the local education authority (LEA):

> To the provision of high quality training and development opportunities that balanced the needs of schools and individuals; that set out the notion of entitlement and equality of access for teachers, support staff and governors, and demonstrated the link between professional development and school improvement.
>
> (Peter Mitchell, quoting Tilbrook, 2012)

Staff development was a key to school achievement. Ruth Heilbronn's contribution shows that at one time in the late 1990s, over 90 per cent of staff were engaged in some form of professional development, a figure that emerged when the school gained *Investors in People* status. Setting learning at the core of teachers' work helped to develop competence and expertise, but more importantly impacted on students' learning, as it provided a model of enthusiasm for and active engagement in learning. Phil Taylor encapsulates this when he talks of gaining a belief from Hampstead 'that teacher growth leads to learner growth, and ultimately to positive outcomes'.

Camden's unified provision for newly qualified teachers and its developmental model of teacher appraisal significantly supported staff learning. Nationally, at the time it took over from the ILEA, this approach to staff development came under pressure for a more market-driven culture, led by targets and externally set priorities. A further context for development was the relationship with the Institute of Education, University of London (IOE), in the provision of a partnership model of school- and university-based initial teacher education, one of four in the country at the time (Ruth Heilbronn). These links fed into the school's high-quality teacher professional development opportunities, such as the school-based MA. While staff development is much more than gaining further accredited qualification, many of the school's teachers engaged in MA studies in which:

> Participants were seeking to learn deeply, and they chose to address such issues as: the quality of learning in classrooms, departments, and whole-school; how matters of creativity and motivation were handled; as well as an examination of what dynamics explained the small number of disaffected teachers who did not engage in a learning culture
>
> (Chris Watkins)

These initiatives have been shared in conferences and publications.

For a non-selective school to be successful in its commitment to the inclusion of all, a strong special needs department must be in place:

> Underpinning the notion of equal worth is the belief that all children are capable of learning so long as lessons are differentiated to meet their individual needs.
>
> (Peter Mitchell)

With its drop-in centre open from 7 a.m. to 6 p.m., Pat Mikhail says: 'As all children were welcomed, I might have one child at the first stages of reading alongside another one writing a book to be published.'

The inclusive aims find their expression in staff working together to develop the curriculum. Staff were appointed who would approach the curriculum with a creative, principled approach and sound subject knowledge, as several of the governors' contributions show, and within the school, all departments were encouraged to reflect on their curriculum offer. In history, for example, Andrea Smith explains:

> We were acutely aware that history was a significant and highly sensitive subject that sought to make sense of the turbulent road to the present, and a subject that permitted and even celebrated the different interpretations of that journey by encouraging logical discussion and debate. Furthermore, it was a subject at the heart of improving communication and other essential literacy skills at all levels.
>
> (Andrea Smith)

The example from Deirdre Broadbent on the redesign of the music curriculum illustrates another rigorous approach and the aim of 'increasing the joy experienced by pupils in their music lessons'.

Creativity

The final area we have chosen to single out from the accounts in this book is that of creativity. Tamsyn Imison states:

> The creative arts and physical education were valued as much as literacy and numeracy, because without the support of a broad, coherent curriculum, many will never become both literate and numerate.

Neela Doležalová endorses this point and indicates the importance of 'the links between creativity, performance, literacy, maths, and science'. Many students' contributions show the range of their arts engagement and the future work they have gone on to achieve in the world of the arts. 'Creativity ran through the school like the words in a stick of rock,' says Mark Mayne, and many of the accounts evidence this creativity in the character and ethos of the school, its curriculum, and the various different kinds of partnerships and collaborations.

As in many successful comprehensive schools, the curriculum was geared to gaining academic qualifications through a broad and balanced curriculum, including arts education, which Jenny Depper saw as integrally related to wider aims of education:

> Our students also learnt socialization and how to be good citizens. Being steeped in cultural literacy and being allowed to communicate and express themselves freely were all within the curriculum and prevailed during the many and varied extracurricular activities led by each and every department.

Jenny evidences the productions and performances that students regularly attended as spectators and participants in London venues, and:

> Extraordinary drama and dance productions, with so many of the students and staff involved. As a result, interaction and mutual admiration between students and staff developed into shared respect within the classroom.

Despite integration, cooperation, and synergies between departments, the individual integrity of the arts subjects was maintained:

> While creativity through cross-curricular links was encouraged, Tamsyn was always adamant that each subject should maintain its

own distinct ethos and approach. This felt particularly important for the arts subjects at this time.

(Mark Mayne)

Mark Mayne goes on to remember his own role in what he describes as 'a healthy competition' among the teachers of the arts subjects:

> We worked hard to upstage each other! I thought that I was doing quite well as head of drama with several big productions, and also the showcasing of some strong examination work in the drama studio, until my colleague, Deirdre Broadbent, head of music, decided to stage an entire opera, with students and staff. It was incredible.

Deirdre Broadbent reminds us what music as part of the broad and balanced curriculum can bring to students and to the whole school community, appreciating and contributing to:

> the joy experienced by pupils in their music lessons. We mainly achieved this by freeing children up, taking risks ... Moving the curriculum away from relying on one type of music to a wider overview, including world music, jazz, pop, and folk made a huge difference to the learning.

As a governor, Rene Branton-Saran was particularly impressed by the range and quality of the performances in music and drama:

> So many [students] were involved. Some staff also played in the school orchestra. The school's commissioned play about the siege of Sarajevo at the time of the Bosnian civil war was outstanding.

Lindsey Rayner remembers this initiative:

> In drama, where the head teacher had organized for Adrian Mitchell and John McGrath to write plays for us and 12 partner schools across the country, the students delivered challenging plays with a maturity that surprised us all.

(Lindsey Rayner)

As a young teacher George Reynoldson attests to the power of creativity in developing initiatives for staff and students, writing about:

> The huge art festival Charlie Cook organized for the whole school off timetable, and he was only in his second year of teaching! It

was really inspiring … We also had strong drama links with both the Tricycle and Hampstead theatres.

Other extra-curricular activities that remain in people's memories as significant aspects of a highly creative approach to education for all students included an innovative *History of Ideas* sixth form induction programme (Andrea Berkeley) and the Rocket Club, where George Reynoldson tells us, 'we launched quite ambitious rockets in the University College school field behind our school. It was often almost too exciting.'

The MA programme we have mentioned was a further example of innovations in teaching and learning that came about as a result of sharing research work in a collaborative partnership. Lindsey Rayner explains how she was enabled to make creative connections in a learning context that have supported her subsequent work as a teacher:

> The process of experimenting, sharing, and disseminating our research was hugely beneficial to me. In subsequent situations I have tried to draw on this as a key driver of school improvement. It was definitely an era and a school where things were allowed to develop organically. Visions emerged rather than being developed through a response to national programmes.

Several contributors relate creativity to freeing up people to take risks, and to the importance of this within a social context, linking this with the kind of education that can best prepare people for future life. Mark Mayne calls this a:

> Creative approach, involving principles of experimentation and connection. In the early years, Hampstead gave me the permission to experiment and connect with other colleagues. Both are about developing optimism for all young people in the face of an increasingly complex and challenging world.

Several teachers also compare this to a top-down kind of approach that they now experience. In reading these accounts it is clear that creativity is linked with vitality, individual expression, and the making of fruitful connections within all the subject areas, for example in science (Mark Everett) and geography (Moira Young).

Finally

These few personal accounts are a small representation of the thousands of fellow colleagues, students, parents, and governors who could have been included if we were not constrained by space and time. We believe these accounts may help to dispel misrepresentations of comprehensive schools, to enable an understanding of a high-achieving, non-selective school, of which there are still many current examples. As Heather Daulphin says in her account:

> I am the successful product of a local comprehensive school, and there is no doubt that with non-selective schools, the mixing of aspirational students with other students raises the aspirations of all and allows social mobility. Such schools force teachers to find ways of addressing all learning needs across the whole spectrum of attainment, and we find in such schools that every child can achieve.

We hope that teachers and parents, and all involved in the vital support and training services now under attack, will take heart from these accounts and their endorsement of the comprehensive ideal of education for all.

Chapter 2
Student voices

Magid El-Bushra

Student 1991–8

Currently opera singer

The best thing I can say about the Hampstead School I attended from 1991 to 1998 has nothing to do with the education I received, which incidentally was second to none – I had friends from local private schools who frequently borrowed my A level notes. Its greatest success was the unbelievable human generosity and investment in the learning process that was afforded to all of us, regardless of academic ability or cultural or social background, by the teachers themselves.

Let's not kid ourselves: Hampstead was rough. As Ms Daulphin used to say, 'Some students go to Oxbridge, and some go to prison'. When I think back to being the only boy in the school dance troupe, giving a class presentation on the artistry of Darcey Bussell, and asking for a CD of Puccini arias as a prize for winning a science quiz, I simply don't know how I ever escaped having the crap kicked out of me.

I remember a girl taking acid during a GCSE biology class and trying to jump off the top floor of the science block. I remember fights of such ferocity they engulfed the whole playground, and I lost count of the number of girls in my year who got pregnant and dropped out. But I also remember Ms Depper crying at an emergency assembly she held when a boy in my year was expelled for selling drugs, telling us how much she cared for us all. I remember Mr Timms devoting an entire lesson to the subject of humility when he discovered that someone in our class was being bullied by another. And I remember Ms Broadbent and Ms Daulphin giving me extra coaching for my university entrance interviews.

Hampstead School was important not only because it was academically non-selective, but also because, due to its catchment area and the fact that it welcomed refugee children from various troubled parts of the world, the atmosphere was truly diverse. In this environment, 'difference' was normalized, and not only did I become accustomed to dealing with different types of people, I also had the chance to be 'different' myself, and to discover that academic aptitude is not the only quality worth striving for in life. I went on from Hampstead to Oxford, which was a great experience academically, but I felt uncomfortable at my college, where there was only one black person in my intake. It reminded me that diversity is one of the key strengths of non-selective education.

After Oxford, I went to the Royal College of Music and am now lucky enough to be able to say that although it's hard, I am doing what I've always wanted to do: I sing in some of the great opera houses and concert halls in Europe. That was always my dream – and that is, in a sense, a success in itself. But somehow it seems as if I have never been able to feel as successful in my life as I felt when I was a student at Hampstead School.

Thinking about my father's childhood in Sudan, about how he used to walk for miles to get to school each morning because he knew that education was the only way he would be able to provide himself with an alternative to herding goats for a living, it makes me feel very lucky to be a product of the state school system, and it fills me with confusion as to how anyone would ever seek to undermine it. The education system here is the jewel in a fading crown, and far more than the welfare system, it's the reason why so many people from other parts of the world want to come and live here. The chance to live in a country where learning is offered free of charge to everyone is a rare gift in the world. Sometimes we need reminding how much it's worth fighting for.

Suhayla El-Bushra

Student 1986–92

Currently screenwriter and playwright

I started at Hampstead comprehensive as a first year and stayed until I finished sixth form. I remember my first day: a self-conscious, half-Sudanese girl who had been back in England for less than two years. I was still getting my head around north London. The primary school I'd been attending had a one-form entry and was predominantly white and middle class. As a latecomer I'd found it hard to fit in.

By comparison, Hampstead had a seven-form entry, with kids from every possible background. It should have been overwhelming and terrifying. It was neither. Everyone was so different that I didn't have to worry about standing out. There were so many other cultures that, for the first time since arriving back in the United Kingdom, I didn't feel self-conscious.

Looking back, this was largely down to the pastoral care we received from our form tutor Rosemary Little and head of year Jenny Depper. The range in our behaviour, expectations, and academic ability was huge, but at no point was I ever made to feel more or less valued than anyone else. I was not a cool kid. I wore strange clothes. I liked homework. My nerdy friends and I spent break times in our tutor room playing hangman. In other schools we might have been picked on mercilessly, but the rest of our form accepted us, as we accepted them. Of course there were conflicts, but these never felt insurmountable. Having taught in a secondary school myself, I now realize what an achievement this was.

I left Hampstead more confident and self-assured than when I arrived, not just academically but socially. For someone who had started off feeling like an outsider, this was no mean feat. I now have a career as a screenwriter and playwright and I owe a lot of it to my schooling, to the drama teachers who inspired me and brought me out of my shell, the English teachers who gave me confidence in my voice and instilled a love of literature, my history teacher, who was also my tutor, who challenged the way I viewed the world. But I also owe it to the rich social experiences I had at school, and the different people I encountered there.

When I returned to secondary school as a drama teacher, I assumed all comprehensives would be like the one I attended, but mixed schools are a dying breed. A form of secondary privatization seems to have occurred, in which middle-class parents flock to the so-called good schools, leaving the underprivileged on their own, tarred with a 'difficult' brush and branded as failing. Society has become more segregated than ever.

I feel incredibly privileged to have had the education I did, and incredibly sad that it's becoming extinct. I worry that my own children will not have the same experience and can't help but feel that something precious has been lost.

John Carruthers

Student 1985–91

Staff 1992–present

Currently network manager at Hampstead School

I started as a Year 7 student and stayed on for one year in the sixth form. I did one year at Kingsway College and then started work as a technician at Hampstead in September 1992. I became network manager with a team of three staff in 2000.

I never had any issues at Hampstead when I was a student. I found friends and got on well. I found academic work difficult, but had lots of support, especially from Pat Mikhail. I remember getting involved with computing and helping Margaret O'Connor. She gave me opportunities to come after school and help other students as well as doing lots of technical tasks, including watering her plants! She was a really warm human being and transformed everyone's attitudes to technology, with the skills and understanding to overcome teachers' and students' fears and get them learning. I was also lucky to work with Phil Taylor, and in our new Independent Learning Centre. Our cross-curricular approach created student and staff autonomy that encouraged a keenness for learning for both staff as well as students.

We were experimenting, and bucking the trends at the time for teaching information and communication technology (ICT) as a discrete subject. We structured things so that technology had to be integral to teaching and learning: like a pen, you don't think about it, you just use it! Once the technology was set up, the positive support Phil and I gave helped people get over their initial fear. We gave lots of support, and this is still a critical part of ICT success. Human interaction is vital. Hampstead gave me the opportunity to take up technical support and ICT as a profession, and the confidence to try different things, such as teaching and training. My own learning is every day and ongoing. I learn from students and staff: *Learning Together, Achieving Together* is a two-way service. Putting ICT at the core of lessons supports and transforms learning and particularly helps those children who, like I did, find academic work difficult. It is far easier to access education and succeed academically using technology.

Hampstead, being a comprehensive school, has allowed me to be where I am today, and the multicultural nature of the school makes it natural for me to think internationally and without prejudice.

James Casey

Student 1985–90

Currently design, ICT and media studies tutor

One September morning, my folks and I trundled down Westbere Road in an old Citroën Dyane to take the plunge into the unknown. After being dropped off, I entered through large gates, past the Victorian building, across the playground into the grounds of the new block, the modern part of the school. I clearly remember a group of bigger boys kicking a ball around. They all looked worldly and tough. I remember feeling very small in this new large ecosystem. Having come from a small Church of England school with a total pupil count of 100, Hampstead School was certainly a new experience.

The teachers were all warm and supportive. Ms Adams was our tutor for the duration of my time at Hampstead, and I also worked closely with Ms Lipinski, our head of year, and Mr Haydn was our support tutor. We had exposure to Mr Warmington and occasionally Ms Imison. All were supportive. Nevertheless, I did find my time at Hampstead School to be tough. Not because of the school, just because I was a troubled young man. I was angry, restless, rebellious, and sad. I struggled with structure, community, and support. I was extremely disruptive in class and would fight to get sent out on most occasions. My most distinctive memory of Hampstead School is the space between the classes, as these spaces became my sanctuary. I would do whatever I could do to derail the class and get sent out and wander the corridors and the grounds. When I think about Hampstead School, my real memories are, in fact, the smells, the textures, and the sounds. I never lost the sensation of running my hands along the wooden beamed handrails in the new block, the chipped paint covering the ring pull levers that were used to open the windows, the feel of the mesh on the back of the old upright pianos.

Unknown to me at the time, Hampstead School had paradoxically become my sanctuary. Although on the surface it may have seemed like I wanted to be elsewhere, I actually never wanted to leave.

I was at Hampstead School from ages 11 to 16. I left shortly before taking my GCSEs in what I remember to be a challenging period. The teachers recognized my difficulties and pulled out all the stops to support me, but it seemed that my issues required more support than was understandably available.

After leaving Hampstead, I eventually found my feet and became involved in design and ICT, an industry I worked in for 18 years. Interestingly, although I was not successful at that early time, I was always interested in education. Years later, good fortune presented me with the opportunity to mentor, coach, and support students and teachers at Hampstead School. This was possibly one of the most cathartic and important moments of my working and personal life, and has inspired me to pursue a path helping young people.

Neela Doležalová

Student 1996–2003

Currently on the Graduate Teacher Training Programme, Institute of Education

It's fair to say I arrived at Hampstead School with no intention, or concept, of being cool. In Year 7 I collected pogs, patterned trousers, commendations, and a few labels to match. In my eyes, school was exciting because I got to meet other kids and 'do stuff'. Somehow Hampstead didn't knock that pre-adolescent enthusiasm out of me – partly by not forcing me to channel it in any specific direction, and partly by teaching us for the sake of learning and not for exams. The only class I remember being set for was GCSE maths. Everything else we learnt together. Hampstead reflected the real world. It didn't block out complexity or conflict. We had freedoms to be political, question, and make noise. In turn, we were expected to justify our opinions and actions.

Looking back, so many teachers put in extra hours to support us. Ms Morrison and Mr Mayne made the drama department a second home to many of us. I spent most evenings at after-school clubs, writing or making plays. Mr O'Hagan taught us formal debating skills: demystifying the language and knowledge of the powerful. Then through debating I learnt what really should matter, and what I really wanted, was 'powerful knowledge' (Young, 2009). Thankfully, knowledge at Hampstead wasn't narrowly defined. As a writer who has internal dyslexic fights every time I have to actually read a book, I'm grateful I was taught to be resourceful. I can now admit, Ms Souzu, that I never actually read *Othello* for A level, but I did listen to it many times – radio, film, stage, friends. The links between creativity, performance, literacy, maths, and science are so important. Now doing my own teacher training (in maths – which is equally as cool), I have many role models to inspire me.

Alison Eardley (now Alison Brolly)

Student 1984–91

Currently senior lecturer in psychology, University of Westminster
I have mixed feelings about my time at Hampstead and the impact it had on my academic career. I value some aspects greatly: the mixed social background and some excellent teachers. I also had some who were not so good. I think I may have succeeded in spite of my secondary education. In fairness to the school, my dyslexia meant that my education at that level was always going to be complicated, and I am not sure what type of environment would have suited me better. It was also a time when a new head teacher had only just arrived, and serious industrial action had begun that did not finish until I was in my fourth year.

The teachers I valued most were the ones who gave me the freedom to explore my own ideas and creativity. I am thinking particularly of Miss Davis, my English teacher for years 1–3, and my A level history teacher, Miss

Little. I also developed an excellent relationship with my art teacher, Miss Harris, with whom I remained in contact for many years. But I also have other memories. In particular, while all my friends were put into the advanced maths class, doing GCSE maths a year early, I was left behind. I was angry, because as far as I was concerned, they were not better at maths than I was. I argued with the school, and while they wouldn't put me into the advanced maths class because I had missed a term of extra work, I was told that I could do the work myself and sit the exam early anyway. So I worked by myself in the class below, sat the exam, and passed with a C. My parents later said that my teacher at the time had told them not to worry if I failed, because I could sit it again with everyone else. That has remained one of my proudest achievements, because I do feel like I taught myself. I am thankful that Hampstead let me sit the exam. It is a flexibility of decision that I appreciate. And I think that it helped consolidate a very strong determination and self-motivation for learning, which has been valuable through the rest of my life.

I was also advised not to do English A level, probably because the quality of my writing wasn't great. I sometimes wonder about this. I went on to do an English degree at university (I changed courses in my first year), which I absolutely loved, and perhaps the A level would have knocked my confidence because my writing skills were poorer, and I would have ended up doing something different. It is also possible that I would have loved it as much as I did my degree, and would have achieved a good grade.

I have often thought that the majority of my secondary school teachers would have fallen off their chairs if someone had told them that I would end up with a PhD and become a lecturer at a university. In fairness, it was Mrs Young who identified, as soon as I started at Hampstead, that the huge difference between my verbal fluency and my writing ability was probably due to dyslexia. I think that with help I could have achieved more than I did at Hampstead, and that the school and the teachers should have been better equipped to identify my ability and to meet the challenges of my different learning styles.

That aside, I have some very fond memories of many teachers, among them Mrs Young, my form tutor and geography teacher throughout my time at Hampstead; of sitting in Miss Harris's room during lunch break; of history lessons with Miss Little, when for the first time I started to really feel like I had good ideas; and of finding out (via a programme on TV) that Mr Judelson, my English teacher, was a secret art collector.

Robbie Ferguson

Student 1994–9

This account was broadcast on Carlton TV, 1998, in Your Shout – a personal view: School Councils *(production Emma White and Joe Farr)*

I am 14 and in Year 10 at Hampstead School. Here we think it is important for all students to have a say in decisions that affect our daily lives. I think this is all students' democratic right.

We have a system called a student council that's made up of students voted in by their classmates to represent them at council meetings. Every class has its own representative so that every student's concerns are voiced. The class reps' ages range from 12 to 19 years old. We meet up twice a term and discuss issues of concern to us all. A member of the student council chairs the meeting and our head teacher sits in, takes notes, and participates when needed. Minutes of the meeting are taken and reported back by the reps at individual class meetings.

Having a school council makes us feel like we have a voice in the running of our school, giving us control over our school lives. In sharing responsibility over how the school runs, we get an insight into how the school operates. We also have two class reps elected at the beginning of each term to attend the governors' meetings, so we get to find out their thoughts on planning for the future.

Issues raised in the student council meeting vary from overcrowded classrooms to lack of variety in the school canteen, as well as the classroom rules that we helped to write. Because we have a say in the rules of the classroom, we are less likely to want to break them. It's good being able to say openly how we feel and to see the problems we have raised being resolved.

Hampstead School is made up of many different cultures and races. Unlike some other schools, we have very few problems of racism or bullying. I really think this is down to the ethos of the school and how the school is united.

I strongly believe that all schools should have a school council like ours. So come on fellow students: stand up for your rights and set up a student council in your school!

Lilah Holywell

Student 1981–8

Currently teacher in charge of drama and expressive arts, academic, Sylvia Young Theatre School

Unlearning the privilege

1981. THIS OLE' HOUSE. STAND AND DELIVER. GHOST TOWN.
When I joined Auden House in September 1981, clutching Miss Barnet's Rubik's cube to my NHS specs like a comfort blanket that I did not want to see beyond, I did not know that I was privileged. What I did know was that getting there in the morning and getting home again took a really long time, and that there were not many people there from my old primary school, Paddington Green. I felt lonely and lost.

1982. COME ON EILEEN. EYE OF THE TIGER. FAME.
For ages, 'school' meant exclusively my own overwhelming everyday experiences lightly leavened with others' anecdotes and half-formed comparisons with Malory Towers and Grange Hill. School was the feelings I felt in response to the things that happened there. Fear, pleasure, excitement, pain, boredom, anxiety, restlessness, joy, frustration, anger, hatred, heartache, heartbreak, remorse, nostalgia, jealousy, disgust, glee, contentment, irritation, amusement, confusion, satisfaction, shame, resentment, bitterness, longing, cynicism, outrage, love, sadness, curiosity. Come in, feelings, sit down.

1983. KARMA CHAMELEON. UPTOWN GIRL. RED, RED WINE.
In letters to pen pals in Canada, Finland, and France, I sought perspective on what this experience was. The Canadian's idea of decent school clothes! Really? The Finn's repetitive day. Not dead of boredom? The French girl's handwriting! Beautiful but exhaustingly consistent! Later burbled exchanges on plasticky C60s with an American who reduced his name to initials. Why was he always on about cars, cars, and the dream of one day maybe someday getting to New York. Unsatisfying.

1984. RELAX. TWO TRIBES. I JUST CALLED TO SAY I LOVE YOU.
Discovering that school itself contained perspectives. Discovery made in English lessons. When it worked it was like losing yourself in a wonderful kaleidoscope, like being refracted, held up to the light, reshaped. Otherworldly. A massive relief to submit to the numinous and let go of the quotidian mechanical knowledge, like bathing in infinity. Whether or not this state was achieved seemed to depend on the material of study. The character of the

teacher could heighten or extend the flight, but the main matter was us and verbal texts. Our flights were powered by verbal texts, engineered by them. Verbal texts, communed with in the magical space of the lesson, the allocated frame of time and space. The matter of words, messengers of mystery, pushed, approved, consecrated. They connected us up. They helped us think. Is that 'me', or not? If I think and feel that it is so, then why? If not, then why not? And what then? What then for me, for us, for everything?

1985. THE POWER OF LOVE. I KNOW HIM SO WELL. FRANKIE.
French, German, Russian, Latin, design and technology, woodwork, metalwork, sewing, cookery, double science, English language, English literature, maths, art, history, geography, physical education, music, religious education, drama. Subjects.

1986. DON'T LEAVE ME THIS WAY. CHAIN REACTION. TAKE MY BREATH AWAY (LOVE THEME FROM *TOP GUN*).
Also, non-structured time in the playground or around the piano in the hall, lunchtimes, break times, vast stretches of free time, there for serendipity. Times when purpose was ordained by authorities, and this other kind of time with peers, practising self-directedness, or absence of purpose. All kinds of people, all hanging out together, day in, day out for years, all part of this same thing, undeniable.

1987. NEVER GONNA GIVE YOU UP. NOTHING'S GONNA STOP US NOW. CHINA IN YOUR HAND.
Lower sixth. We liked the sound of that. It had dignity. It separated us from those little ones. We'd done our time, embarrassing time, down there in the playground. We were seniors now and never needed to go through that again. We barely notice them. We are in the common room now, with the oak banisters. Be gone, small people. A timetable with lots of nice empty space on it is this year's thing. Somewhat alarming but just, you know, read around your subjects in that blank time. It's A levels, for goodness sake. Everyone knows that you have to read around your subjects. And music.

1988. I SHOULD BE SO LUCKY. THE ONLY WAY IS UP. NOTHING'S GONNA CHANGE MY LOVE FOR YOU.
Upper sixth. Four people from Hampstead apply to Oxbridge, two boys, two girls. In the interview, when they ask which texts I am studying for English A Level, I genuinely manage to forget 'bloody *Emma*', as that book has become known at home, after the new young A level teacher thought that we would like it if she showed us her holiday snaps of places a bit Jane Austen relevant, over several lessons, as, you know, a way into the text, instead of, you know,

teaching us what was important and interesting about the book. Tedious book. Hilarious unconscious excision of it. They seemed to like that I liked *Paradise Lost* and Coleridge, and that we had covered Chaucer, and that I loved but did not understand *The Four Quartets*. They asked whether I spoke German. No I didn't, and why on earth would that be of any possible relevance (I think), and yes, I did a year of it, and how useful it could be for the study of Old English I suppose (I say). The two girls get in. Maryam is accepted to study earth sciences in a faraway college and I do not even know what that subject is, so how is it possible that she knows it so well that it is about to become her future.

1989–2000. Everything I Do (I Do It For You). Love Is All Around. I Will Always Love You.

Oh there *are* public school kids in the world. They exist, and here they all are! How unsettling. And there is a subject here called PPP and it involves 'experimental' psychology. That doesn't sound very nice. I would hate to cut up frogs and stuff! And you can do a degree here in Chinese! Well did you ever! And who on earth would want to do that? And what A levels did I do and what did I do in my Year Out and I come from a state school? In London? Wow! Actually, wow! And your dad does what? And you are dressed like what? It's OK. You're in a college that takes an unusually high proportion of state school applicants. You'll be fine. Cling on to CS Lewis and Tolkien. You'll be fine. And you have to learn Old English. Well, not exactly learn it, more like memorize modern English translations of the few existing texts and then recite them on paper in the summer exam. Oh yes, that counts towards your degree. And critical theory. Terry's gone but the new guy seems alright. Oh, you write. That's good. Here's where you can put on that play you wrote over the summer. There will be an audience and your friends can be in it. And I'm sure you can also act and direct, have a go. What are you going to do after Oxford? Well here's the Milk Round. It's where employers try to get you to join their company. Oh, management consultants, mostly, and law firms. And if you get into doing anything that involves following your talents with a passion, they'll call you a 'hack'. Just don't worry about it. Then a teaching degree at the Institute of Education, work in different schools in London and elsewhere, and at the Medical Foundation, and a Master's in psychoanalytic developmental psychology at the Anna Freud Centre/UCL with distinction, and a thesis on using stories in group work with unaccompanied adolescent refugees and how we can show that it works.

2001–13. Umbrella. Crazy. Bleeding Love. Is This the Way to Amarillo?
Since 2001, I have helped to train and educate hundreds of children and young people in theatre, film, radio, and television, in the role of 'teacher in charge of drama and expressive arts, academic' at Sylvia Young Theatre School, based in central London. There is freedom to choose the texts I use in my classroom/studio. There is freedom to adapt the teaching styles and techniques that I use in my classroom/studio, within my capabilities in response to the live situations that I encounter minute by minute, within the predictability of the pattern of how we have done things before and the imperative of what to accomplish within the curriculum. There is freedom to practise responsiveness and to effect tiny transformations in tiny steps, often backwards. When it works there is a feeling of grace and connectedness, which is like a pure, clear, resonant note. When the light goes on it is tangible and utterly beautiful. When it goes off I will fall on my face. Some will laugh, some will help me up, and I will try again.

Hampstead was for everyone, not for an apartness-perpetuating, people-like-us mentality. And the amazing thing is, that for this privilege, my parents did not have to pay a single penny. How remarkable is that? My parents did not have to maintain a certain level of income to be able to afford school fees, in order to maintain a sense of specialness. My parents did not have to maintain a certain lifestyle in order to afford school fees in order to maintain a sense of self-worth based on separateness and caste and fear. It meant that they could work in low-paid jobs, like teaching.

I wish that we could stabilize and transfer and normalize and perpetuate the human realizations that make us connect and care, and I think we can, but to do so we have to give up many of the things that we currently believe necessary to our happiness. In reality, status anxiety is a sickness, and 'affluenza' can be cured, and the rewards are justice, grace, and sustainable life on this planet. I was so lucky and so privileged to live that inclusive, difficult reality at Hampstead.

David Ruebain

Student 1978–81

Currently chief executive of the Equality Challenge Unit
It was the end of the summer of 1978. I don't remember much except that I was quite terrified. I was just a 16-year-old boy, healthy but with a noticeable disability that affected all my limbs, and hence my mobility and dexterity. For those of us born with our impairments, it was just another feature of ourselves, but for others it was often upsetting, sad, and even a tragedy.

Consequently, this is often what we believed of ourselves. This was a time before the idea of integration of disabled people was largely accepted, and I had been at mostly so-called special schools, apart from two years at a regular primary school, and had just left a special boarding school where I had been for five years.

Things weren't good. My mother had died when I was nine years old and my father really wasn't up to looking after me. Both my parents were immigrants and didn't really have much of a network of support. I hated boarding school and also hated home. And I had few friends, certainly not nearby. But worse, although I was considered bright, I left boarding school with a total of two O levels – English language and maths – both at grade C. What was I to do?

In my final year of boarding school, I had resolved to continue my education back in London with a view to doing A levels. In the absence of an involved parent, I wrote to the secondary schools in what was then known as Division 2 of the ILEA, which was Camden and Westminster, asking if I could come and do A levels. Most replied that this was not how it was done! I was supposed to ask my father to write to the ILEA. This wasn't possible – he simply wasn't up to it. However, Hampstead School wrote a different letter.

Ms Gittins, deputy head, replied, inviting me to visit. I did and when I told her that I had failed most of my O levels, she warmly encouraged me to come anyway and join the lower sixth form. So there I was, the odd-looking, chubby, foreignish kid who had no idea about proper secondary schools, feeling profoundly immature compared with the mass of lively, independent kids before me.

I did O level retakes and did OK. I then did A levels and also did OK. With the encouragement of teachers at Hampstead, I applied and got in to Oxford University, where I subsequently went to study politics, philosophy, and economics. But more importantly, my three years at Hampstead were transformative. I learnt how to be human, not 'disabled'. I made enduring, deep friendships that remain. I had more fun than I had ever had, including acting in a fabulous production of *Joseph and the Amazing Technicolor Dreamcoat,* and I was never, ever bullied. I also avoided the care home that was all that was expected of me.

I think that I was lucky with the staff and students of Hampstead, but more importantly, I don't think that this could have happened except in a comprehensive. Nowhere else could I have been treated as a person and not a category, and nowhere else could I have been thought about so particularly. I know that it wasn't all perfect, although compared to the dismal hopelessness of special school it seemed like it, and being sociable enough to get on with most people greatly helped, but the principle of non-separation that ran through the comprehensive ideal was key.

Nandi Simpson

Student 1986–91

Currently operations manager for the Infection, Immunity, and Inflammation Programme, National Institute of Health Research, University College London Hospitals Biomedical Research Centre
I arrived at Hampstead School in 1986, having completed the first year at another north London comprehensive, switching because I was being bullied at my first secondary school. I left Hampstead in 1991 at the end of the sixth form, to go to university.

I remember a very positive atmosphere at the school – as pupils we were encouraged to get involved in things that interested us. I studied the sciences at A level and, thinking back, remember a very open-door environment, with teachers engaging in conversations around the subject and facilitating extra-curricular projects and activities. I also remember enjoying tutorials with our form tutor, where we would have discussions on a range of subjects. We didn't have a formal general studies course, but I guess these tutorials were providing us with life skills.

I feel as if secondary school was such a formative experience it is tempting to say I learnt virtually everything I know there, but to narrow it down, I think that the key thing I took with me from the school was self-belief. I had the feeling while there that it was expected we would be excellent. I left Hampstead with, frankly, terrible A level results, and completely undeterred by this, continued on to my first choice of degree course at my first choice of university. I think having come from a school environment where I felt I was expected to be good at the subjects I was studying, it was difficult to dent my belief that I could achieve whatever I wanted to achieve.

Since leaving school I have been studying and working in my chosen field, infectious disease research. After my undergraduate degree, I obtained an MSc and was awarded my PhD in Molecular Microbiology by Imperial College London. I currently work as the operations manager for the infection, immunity, and inflammation programme at the UCLH/UCL Biomedical Research Centre. I've worked in academic institutions, as well as briefly in the civil service, and although the majority of my career has been in London, I spent three and a half years living in Paris as a post-doctoral research fellow.

For me, one of the major advantages of non-selective education is that it instilled in me the idea that everyone has strengths and weaknesses, and an appreciation of the variety of strengths found in others. I completed my primary school education in Zimbabwe, where the education system was based on a very traditional and conservative English model. One of the contrasts I found coming from that background to a comprehensive school was that the environment at Hampstead was very much less competitive, which made learning a less fearful experience. In general, I value non-selective education because I believe it is more egalitarian. I find working in a Russell Group university that among my peers, the privately educated outnumber those of us from comprehensive schools. I do feel proud to have come from a comprehensive school.

Megan Smith

Student 1993–8

Currently business development and brand partnerships manager for a leading publisher

I chose to go to Hampstead mainly because it seemed a natural progression from the local primary school to go to the local secondary school, which all my friends did too. In fact, I am one of the very few people I know from London who can say that from the age of two until 16 I had more or less the same people in my class throughout. There were no exams or interviews to get into the school, which meant it encouraged everybody from West Hampstead and Cricklewood, despite which road you grew up in or what your household income or class might be, let alone how academic you were. It would give me an opportunity to be educated within my home area among a broad spectrum of people.

I would describe the student body while I was there as diverse culturally, but simultaneously local and representative of that pocket of London and its communities. Also, I knew Hampstead offered not just curriculum learning, but learning through a wealth of other activities. It had a good reputation for the arts, which were my particular interest, and I took part in a great many plays and musicals, was also a member of the choir, and later joined the jazz orchestra. There was even a sprung gym, allowing the school to offer dance, and I was able to take it as an additional GCSE. On top of this, I sat on the school council and also participated in Socratic dialogue discussions. After Hampstead I completed my A levels and went on to study at Manchester University, where I achieved a first class honours degree in English literature and won a scholarship to continue on to an MA in the European languages and cultures department. After finishing my postgrad, I pursued a career in publishing, and now work for a leading publisher as their business development and brand partnerships manager. Outside work I continue to be involved in many activities, but have recently taken a break from most things to have my first child.

But Hampstead wasn't just a school I went to; it is a culture and community I belong to, still. Looking back, by far the best thing about it is its degree of loyalty among students and deep-seated friendships across year groups, which still remain today. Before the existence of social networking sites or even the internet itself, Hampstead students had a strong sense of community, and to this day many of us, and by that I mean hundreds, not tens, meet regularly. I would describe those people as close or good friends rather than simply acquaintances. My confidence and 'never-mind, can-do' attitude along with any successes I have had since leaving, I can attribute to the network of friends I met there and our collective interest in promoting one another, no matter who we are or what challenges we might face in our personal life. Hampstead School, in my opinion, breeds a student not just ambitious for himself, but for his classmates too. Normally that sort of networking is attributed to old Etonians rather than the students of inner-city comprehensives. Among my friends from those school days, I know lawyers, teachers, journalists, actors, artists, academics, architects, bankers, entrepreneurs, and a host of other successful people. So the school motto was actually very typical of the student: *Learning Together, Achieving Together*.

Luke Storey

Student 1997–2001

Currently DJ, actor

Hampstead School felt both dangerous and safe. Kids came from everywhere, every class, culture, and religion. It was real life from the start, strong in the arts, and I had two favourite teachers who pushed me. I remember best Miss Morrison, my drama teacher, who saw something in me that others didn't. When I was at my most unteachable, she suggested in exasperation that I just 'go off and get famous then'. It was a provocation that stayed with me. I remember Tamsyn [Imison] very well – not many like her, she had authority, but was calm and gentle with it – she had all our respect.

David Sunderland

Student 1984–91

Currently performance monitoring adviser, UNAIDS, Geneva

I lived 10 minutes' walk away from the school. During the summer holiday of 1991, after leaving, I worked as a laboratory assistant in the science department, helping to prepare materials for lessons in the coming year. As I succeeded in obtaining a place and studying geography at Cambridge University, the experience at Hampstead served me well academically, and I have good memories of my learning experience. The teachers had a down-to-earth and inclusive approach that I felt was well embodied by Moira Young, my favourite (and geography) teacher, who inspired me in the subject and encouraged me in my studies. The 'interest in the world' inherent within geography has continued with me, and serves me in my career with international charities and the United Nations. Hampstead School helped me to excel academically and also, through the comprehensive system, study with and make friends across a wide range of backgrounds. Much more than the grades from my exams, this has helped me to interact and feel at ease with people and situations in many different contexts, something I think I would lack to an extent if I had attended a public school.

While serving the needs of a broad range of students, perhaps Hampstead School did not have enough capacity (in the 1980s) to encourage more activities for students. I studied Latin at GCSE, rather than a modern language, being embarrassed to speak in class. Yet I have gone on to learn French, Portuguese, and Spanish, take up singing, and develop a considerable amateur dramatic portfolio, including writing, directing, and acting in a number of plays, despite never excelling or taking an interest in music or drama. Perhaps this can partly be explained by being a timid adolescent devoted more to studies than other activities, but I know my experience at Hampstead School gave me a good base for developing independent learning and activities. My memories of the wider school organization are more limited, but I remember a sense of a safe learning environment that was representative of the local area.

Ediba-Bakira Trbonja-Kapic

Student 1994–6

Currently personal assistant to HM ambassador, Sarajevo

It has defined me. War, being a refugee was just the start of it. Leaving my country, family, and friends was the development. Landing in the United Kingdom, London at age of barely 17 was the determiner.

Nowhere to go and no one you know. From the town of 18,000 population in total, to the capital of millions: foreign language, foreign cultures, strange ways, stranger food and hosts' insufficient knowledge of the ordeal my country, in the heart of Europe, is going through at the verge of the new millennium. Bosnians are a breed different to British – we cling on to our families, we try not to part, ever. And then something like war happens and you are scattered, made to flee, leave all you ever known and cared for behind, no turning back. I left my mother a refugee in Croatia, caring for my sister-in-law and two-year-old nephew who fled besieged Sarajevo; left my two brothers in Sarajevo, fighting for what is left of the country; my father, the pain of pains – locked up in a concentration camp run by almost the same imagination as those in the Second World War – a doctor held in camp just so he couldn't help those in need.

Lost.

But you have to be lost to be found – and this is what I was. Luck had it that I landed in Hampstead School, only school in the world with the heart and soul. Only school that wanted to know more, to go beyond the news reports and wanted to search the trouble in detail, to know what it is that made us so lost and so alone.

Soon they learnt that besides the worry about your loved ones, lack of any information of them, news of devastation, death and loss back home, we had to face the struggle of day-to-day life – how you get to school, how you understand what they tell you with little English or English not good enough for school. How you find a place to live, how you pay the bills, how you find what you need in the shop, what you do with the food they give you – it was only yesterday that your mum cooked for you.

If I was to go back in time I would ask for the same support I was given. It was perfect, aimed and tender. Teachers were there to give you the confidence and knowledge; soon I could hear myself saying 'Miss, Miss, look at me, I made it through the day and looking forward to the next one'. Shoulder to cry on, mother to hug, father to keep safe, friend in need, your guide, your conscience, your pillar – that's what my teachers at Hampstead were.

Students, my peers, were there to show that even the tender teen age won't stop them being deep, compassionate, caring, understanding; that they'd rather give their free time to us scruffy and unknowing refugees than go clubbing – determined to get past our face barriers saying 'stay away, I don't need you'; recognizing the grave need for acceptance, blending in and being one of the group; and giving it all, selflessly and with passion only known to youth.

This perfect match of teachers' knowledge and desire to help students; students' need to go beyond, and refugees' need to survive, came together in what was Children of the Storm at Hampstead School [a charity to support child refugees in North London]. It was simple but as effective as the toughest aid agency; kind as the best peer support group, and as helping as the top counselling facility.

I had trouble getting out of the house. It was hard to find the purpose. It was hard to face a class full of unknown. It was hard to know the subject but to lack a word and be too embarrassed to speak up. I would get a call. 'Where are you?', it said. 'So, you missed a lesson, come to next one, we are all waiting for you'. Embarrassment of disappointing those who show you they care becomes larger than one of not knowing the word. So you attend. You get to know all the words and you get to show you are actually smart.

I was hungry – it was hard to live on £32 per week, pay bills and eat. But then there would be a box of food after lessons, something new for me to try, something I probably don't have back home, way to give me food without making me feel desperate. Even better, I would be given money and asked to shop for myself – lesson in English they said, and I got to keep all that I bought.

I had nowhere to live. Finding rental agency to trust you, a refugee from a God-forsaken country was impossible, even with a deposit – not that I had one – but a teacher vouching, concrete, solid-weight guarantee, always made it possible to get a place you can call your own.

I had trouble making friends – they didn't understand my suffering, plus, I had all those friends back home that I would surely be betraying by making new ones. But no, Children of the Storm kids wouldn't give up – they would come to your home, they would find out when your birthday is and celebrate it. They'll come to do maths with you; they'll invite you to their home; they'll be fun; they'll be real friends – and you had to let them, left with no choice.

I am a grown-up now. I have a job. I have a family. I have half returned. I am back in my country but not quite back to my hometown. I visit. Some people there still don't want to accept that war is long over and insist on disliking me because of my name, my nationality. But that will pass with time as well. It has to. We'll move on and our children will not even know what their parents fought for. And they shouldn't – so as to avoid revenge for whatever cause was lost on their parents during this horrible and unnecessary war.

I am a grown-up now. I have morals, principles, and standards. I manage to stick to them. I function. I get up in the morning on time, I go to work, I have holidays, I spend time with my friends. I am happy. I don't need a reason to be reminded life is worth living.

I am a grown-up now. I still have the teenage refugee in me. And I wouldn't let her go, ever. I have her to balance me, to remind me how life can be, how people can be. Not the bad people. How good people can be. How you can wake up one day and from being your daddy's princess, end up a stamp in Lunar House in Croydon. How you can land on someone's doorstep, needy and devastated and how they'll open the door, take you in without even asking your name. Give you shelter, food, clothes, cover all your logistical earthly needs.

How they'll love you, cherish your memories with you, be silent when you cry, smile when you laugh, listen to your stories of back-home as if it was a place from a fairy tale, stay up with you for hours at night when news reports were particularly bad and the killed were counted in hundreds, thousands. How they'll be there to let you be part of their life, take you in fully, letting you crash on the couch when you can't bear the emptiness of your own place. How they'll teach you that a cup of tea goes a long way, solving almost all issues, and instantly making you feel better.

How they will show you what a person should be like. How human should be to human. How it should be.

Hampstead School, Children of the Storm, staff, students – they were my making, my determiner. They set my morals, my standards, my values. They showed me that one can always do more and better if he chooses; that it is worth taking time to scratch beneath the surface, open a whole new world where everyone learns and gains.

I am a grown-up now. But forever the Child of the Storm, and mighty proud of it.

Chapter 3
Parent and governor voices

Rene Branton-Saran

Governor early 1970s–2000

Formerly teaching and research at City of London Polytechnic until retirement in 1986. Publications cover secondary schools policy, school teachers' salaries policy, and school governing bodies and Socratic dialogue. Facilitated Socratic dialogues at Hampstead School and abroad, including Lithuania, Bulgaria, Germany, and Mexico.

I began as a governor as a Labour Party appointment, when Labour governors were the majority of political appointees, in line with council representation. During my time a new law reduced the number of politically appointed governors and increased parent and staff representation. I had been an opponent of 11+ selection, an active supporter of comprehensive schools, a committee member of Camden CASE (now Campaign for State Education), and a governor of a Hampstead feeder primary school. My long experience of being a primary and secondary governor enabled me to see the full educational process for children, from nursery through to secondary at age 18.

I was chair of governors before Tamsyn Imison was appointed head teacher in 1983, and I had already been involved in other staff appointments, but none of these equalled in importance that of appointing a new head. The early 1980s were a difficult time, as long industrial action by teachers discouraged headship applications. London was badly affected by this, and we had not appointed on two previous occasions. When the third pile of application forms reached us, I saw immediately that Tamsyn's stood out – she had not applied in the first two rounds. She had an unusual track record, not having gone into teaching after graduating. It was clear to me that Tamsyn would bring to Hampstead a wide range of human and professional skills. The appointment was duly made with the support of ILEA's councillors, and I can honestly say that from that day onwards, the school changed and improved. The previous head had come from a grammar school background and brought with him the attitudes prevalent in a selective education system.

Staffing was a challenge, and some weaknesses not addressed by the previous head were now tackled urgently, as the head set in motion removal of dead wood from the staff. Sometimes this involved rather drawn-out industrial tribunal hearings and needed iron resourcefulness and much time. In these staffing matters, the inspectorate, and I as chair, fully supported the head.

It was one of the strengths of the school that Tamsyn had a democratic yet strong style of leadership, and that the senior management team consulted frankly on major school issues. Yet there are always issues that initially the head needs to discuss in confidence with someone not directly involved, who is like an 'insider outsider'. In some contexts the inspector may exercise this role. I saw it as one of the roles of the chair to have a listening ear and to support the head over sensitive issues, but to challenge her assessment and, where appropriate, offer a different perspective. In contrast, some of the newer Labour governors saw it as the governors' role to control the head. In my view this is an unrealistic basis for running a school effectively. Governors are volunteers and usually meet only twice a term. By contrast, the school staff are better informed and have to manage everyday tasks. What governors can do is to discuss and agree strategic policies, usually drafted by staff and/ or the head, on matters like school organization, the school development plan, behaviour management, and the setting up of a student school council.

Some of the disagreements over how to exercise the powers of the governors can be seen in the context of Labour Party politics in the Borough of Camden and in the country at that time. This was when leading Labour politicians broke away from the Labour Party and founded the SDP (Social Democratic Party). At this point another Labour governor became chair, and I was elected vice-chair. Later, when the number of Labour appointees was reduced, I became a co-opted governor, which actually gave me more independence.

How governors worked

The twice-termly meetings of governors were quite large (up to 20), so we did much of our work through sub-committees. During Tamsyn's headship, I had particular involvement with the salaries sub-committee, having made an extensive study of the Burnham salary scales for schoolteachers, using a grant from the Social Science Research Council (SSRC). This enabled me to contribute to pay policy at Hampstead in the late 1980s. For a considerable period I chaired the governors' salaries sub-committee and drafted Hampstead's pay policy.

Other sub-committees covered, for example, appointments of staff, staff and student discipline, and finance. In addition, governors were attached to one or two departments in the school – mine were history and geography. Our task was to visit the department, get to know the staff, observe (definitely *not* inspect) lessons, and give feedback to the head of department. We also acted as ambassadors for our departments on the governing body. On the face of it this sounds formal and perhaps boring, but far from it. It meant that as a governing body we acquired closer knowledge of what was going on, how students were taught, and how student–staff relationships worked at grassroots level.

Over the years I chaired the staff and the student disciplinary committees. These were not my most favourite jobs, but had to be done with care and by ensuring fair dealing for all involved. Even though we had a total staff of well over 100 and around 1,300 students, the number of times disciplinary committees had to sit was very low. Usually the school found other ways of dealing with staff and student difficulties, helping people to mend their ways and improve. For a large inner-city comprehensive, we had a very low student exclusion rate, because the school's pastoral system worked well with students and parents.

I soon saw, when parents turned up at the disciplinary hearing of their youngster, that for the few students who really struggled, it was often the parents who needed support, so that they could better support their daughter or son. On the staff side there were very few disciplinary cases. Some staff could see they were not in the right job in this vibrant and very demanding school, and left of their own accord. The main difficulty for all involved, especially for the busy head, was that disciplinary proceedings absorbed a huge amount of time.

Sharing the Positive

Many governors regularly attended school functions like concerts, performances of plays, and school fairs. The achievements of students in music and drama were impressive, and so many of them were involved. Some staff also played in the school orchestra. The school's commissioned play about the siege of Sarajevo at the time of the Bosnian civil war was outstanding.

Another involvement for governors was helping at the twice-yearly individual student work reviews. Students came with their parents for 20-minute sessions and brought their work and their own targets for the next six months, which they had discussed with their subject and form teachers.

This regular feature for all students was very demanding in energy and time for the teaching staff, and governors who participated were always welcomed.

I remember being almost petrified of not being sufficiently sensitive. One of our refugee students from former Yugoslavia told me that one of her targets was to improve her English. Trying to encourage her, I asked her whether she had made friends among the students who were native English speakers. 'No', she responded. Having gathered that at home she conversed in her mother tongue, I said that making friends among the English mother-tongue students would help her with her target. Suddenly she said: 'I don't want to make new friends ... most of my former friends are dead'. I was speechless and apologized for having pressed and upset her.

An outstanding experience was a one-day Socratic dialogue session, which I was invited to conduct mainly for students on the school council. This was an initiative of the charity the Society for Furtherance of Critical Philosophy (SfCP), of which I was secretary. At the end of a dialogue about equal rights for girls and boys, the students came up with the question of whether they themselves treat their teachers equally, particularly with relation to female and male teachers. In another dialogue, 'Is bullying a fact of life?', they drew up two lists – the first outlined how the bullied could protect themselves; the second gave points of advice for bullies. To me this revealed a group of youngsters who cooperatively exercised their sharp minds to work out really good answers to major questions concerning life in school. Tamsyn attended all these sessions, and the young people accepted her during the dialogue sessions as 'Tamsyn'. Outside the sessions she remained Mrs Imison, our head teacher. The youngsters were not in the least intimidated by discussing important issues with, or in the presence of, their head teacher. For me, that really reflected the ethos of the school.

Leaving the two Camden school governing bodies was a big wrench, but when in 2000 Tamsyn retired as a head teacher, I thought it the right time for me to go. Getting involved in the appointment of a new head and then resigning soon afterwards would be unfair to the new person. So, shedding a few tears, I went! In acknowledgement of my commitment to comprehensive education, I am really glad to still be around to contribute my thoughts to this important book.

Charles Chadwick CBE

Governor 1992–2000

Civil servant from the early 1970s. British Council officer in Nigeria in 1972, and worked in Kenya, Brazil, Canada, and Poland. Novelist.

I became a governor of Hampstead School in 1992, shortly after retiring from the British Council. I had no direct experience of comprehensive education, but in facilitating educational exchanges with other countries, I had kept up to date with the educational scene in Britain by reading *The Times Educational Supplement*.

I was a governor for about eight years. It was an experience for which I shall always be very grateful. What I best remember is the distinctive spirit of the school and the sense of commitment that was shared by teachers and students alike. For example, when recruiting new teachers, the ultimate question was how well he or she would fit in. It was not only a matter of dedicated professionalism. That went without saying. There was also the need to look for other qualities less easy to define: originality, warm-heartedness, a lightness of touch and, as important as anything, a sense of humour that could see the gladness in things. It was urbanity without solemnity. (Once upon a time, it might have been described as a kind of gaiety.)

I recall with admiration the attention given to students who had gone off the rails or were in danger of doing so. Exclusion meetings were conducted with great thoroughness in searching for the causes of behaviour and finding ways of bringing students back into the fold. The school's ethos did not allow the smallest suggestion that any child could be written off. I took part in meetings with parents and students with disciplinary problems that combined warning with planning the way ahead. In such a fully comprehensive school, there were children who came from troubled homes who needed to believe they belonged to the school family no less than anyone else. In all this, the care and compassion were contained within a framework of order and discipline, and a belief in whatever excellence students were capable of. Any good school would doubtless express its aims and purpose in similar terms. They have become clichés. At Hampstead they were embodied.

What part could governors play to help the school maintain its standards? It is perhaps generally the case that if the leadership of a school is strong and purposeful, the less need there is for the active involvement of a governing body much beyond reviewing plans and progress at periodic board and committee meetings. The key is the relation between the head teacher and the chair of governors who carries ultimate responsibility for the school's reputation. At Hampstead the relationship was strong, and at meetings one never had the feeling that there was tension or uneasiness under the surface. On the contrary I do not recall an occasion when, whatever opinions individual governors might have expressed, there was any sense of real dissension. With the chair setting the tone, the confidence of the governors in the head and her leadership team was, I think, unqualified. Without that confidence and unity, one can easily imagine schools running into severe loss of morale and all kinds of other difficulties.

So what was there for governors to do? First, the governing body had to be there: as a representative link with the wider and parental community, and as an accountable reserve of authority – a 'fleet in port'. But there were also tasks to be performed. I have mentioned appointment and exclusion meetings. There were other occasions that required the participation of governors. Having retired, I was readily available to carry out these tasks. Most governors have jobs to do that require skills (such as finance, business management, or curriculum development), which are directly useful to the school. With no such skills, at least I could offer my time more or less on demand. It was always rewarding to do so.

Governors were encouraged to take an interest in subject departments. My department was English (in which I had a degree). I have heard of schools where teachers regard the involvement of governors as intrusive. This was never so in my experience. I was always made to feel welcome. It was not interference but a mark of interest. These departmental links were important in giving governors an idea of what was actually happening at the school, what teachers felt about what they were doing, and generally keeping one's finger on the pulse – thereby lending authority to their views and queries at meetings and on other, less formal occasions.

A task that gave me particular pleasure was taking part in work reviews at which students' performance was discussed with them and targets were set for the future. This personal contact with students, however brief, gave me a sense of the very wide range of their ability and background, and also of how they exemplified the distinctive spirit of the school. The same sense of pride and belonging was evident in musical, theatrical, and other events.

In short, I was given opportunities to get to know the school, and made to feel that that pride was something I too could share.

Angella Hodgson

Parent governor 1994–7

My two daughters attended the school: Santina Hodgson-DeSilva gained a B.Ed in early years education at the Institute of Education, University of London, and is shortly to start teacher training. She works as a primary school teaching assistant and is a staff governor. Krishana completed an MA at California State, Los Angeles, on a tennis scholarship and worked as a professional tennis coach, having gained the US qualifications.

I had long known Hampstead School; my best friend from secondary school lived on the same road as the school. One of the reasons I wanted my children to go there was because I felt the head was a strong leader. This was something I desired as a parent: a head with the vision and the strength to provide and maintain a strong school that ensured an environment in which students could learn.

My elder daughter had only been at Hampstead School for a few weeks when a vacancy came up for a parent governor. I was at university at the time as a mature student, undertaking a BA in education and sociology. I was also a single parent with two school-age children. I wanted to apply for the post of parent governor, but was concerned on various levels – time commitment, skills – and would anyone vote for me, as I only knew one or two parents at the school? I did stand and was elected. A couple of weeks before the first meeting, I received two large packages in the mail. When I opened them, I realized that I had underestimated the amount of work involved. It was clear that at Hampstead there was an expectation that governors would commit fully to the role, and that they would be included in a wide range of activities, including the running of the school as well as the long-term strategic planning.

On the day of the first meeting Rene Saran and another governor, Charles Chadwick, immediately put me at ease. They gave me a quick explanation of the meeting process and made sure I had the key ingredient – a cup of coffee!

What really impressed me was how governors were integrated into the daily workings of the school. For example, each governor was assigned a subject area, based on their own outside expertise or interests. I chose languages. Having previously lived in Brazil for a short time, I had become well aware of the benefits of speaking another language.

The role included an expectation where possible to attend staff meetings, observe teaching, speak to pupils, and report back to the governing body any issues related to the area to which we were assigned. It was clear to me that governors were conscientious and enthusiastic. Meetings often overran because no one wanted to rush the agenda or curtail important discussion. Other governors gave a lot of their own time and expertise – for example, one governor investigating a new student sports facility had many meetings with architects and planners.

Both formal and informal training was offered. I particularly found the informal on-site training fruitful, as it allowed me to learn in the context of school. On one occasion I had undertaken observations of the language department, and when writing up my findings, I had named a teacher whom I had been particularly impressed with. Having sent my report for the next governors' meeting, I was asked by the head to come in to discuss the report. Although the head was very busy, the fact that she was willing to meet with me to go over protocol and the reasons for the various procedures such as confidentiality was a sign of the professionalism, and showed that governors were part of the school, and not outsiders who merely rubber-stamped decisions.

At times I found it difficult as a governor to know what best to do. Through my degree in education I was aware of how the government changes affected families and students. At the time, the government had brought in a new curriculum that in my view limited choice for students. As a result Hampstead School required students to take double science, which meant that they could not take two languages. Although the other parent governor raised the issue of those students who did not desire a career in science, I was swayed by the arguments of why it was easier to learn a new language at A level than catch up with a science subject. With hindsight I wish I had believed in my own judgement and life experience more. However, although decisions were not easy, a decision had to be reached, and the focus of the discussions was always what was best for the student. We were required by the government to deliver the national curriculum, and only had a limited amount of choice in what else we could offer the students.

One of the activities I loved about being a governor was selection of new staff. I felt this role was really important, as teachers play such a fundamental role in evoking the motivation and passion for a subject area that can stay with students for the rest of their lives. It was particularly wonderful when a job was advertised nationally for a head of department, and the successful applicant was a member of staff who would gain a promotion. The school was meeting the aspirations of not just students but also staff. The interview process at Hampstead was ahead of its time. The rigorous selection procedure included being interviewed by the students. Interviewees were required to deliver a lesson to a group of mixed-ability students who then assessed the teacher based on their own agreed criteria. It was not until some years later that I heard about other schools and colleges adopting this process.

Sophia MacGibbon

Parent 1981–9

Daughters Rosa and Ellen attended the school

I thought Hampstead was a fantastic school, the nearest to a real comprehensive that I've come across, in that it had a true academic and social mix. I fought for my girls to go there, and I never regretted that choice. It was terrific for girls, a fact reflected in the amazing take-up at A level of craft design and technology (CDT); I think one of the best rates in London. I think my children had an excellent academic education and teachers who often went beyond the call of duty. Both Rosa and Ellen had Mrs Bromnick, who gave them amazing support, often giving them extra tuition at the weekends.

I also think that attending a school with such a social mix was an excellent education in its own right, and taught them so much about people. As a consequence they have both done well in the world of work at managerial levels, as they are able to get the most out of their staff through empathetic appreciation of their strengths and appropriate strategies to help them overcome weaknesses.

Rosa said Hampstead School taught her how to think, whereas most schools seemed more geared to teaching children how to work.

John Mann

Posts included secretary, Schools Council for Curriculum and Examinations 1978–83; director of education, London Borough of Harrow 1983–8.

Parent of Susan, now a senior teacher, International School Mexico City, and David, a senior human resource manager of an international IT company, currently based in Switzerland

We came to London in 1978 with an eight-year-old daughter and seven-year-old son, and few preconceptions about the kinds of schools we would find in London, or their quality. School catchment areas played no part in our choice of where to settle, but we came from Sheffield with some baggage. I had been the city's deputy education officer for 11 years, heavily involved in the evolution of a highly participative system of inclusive comprehensive schools. Margaret was deputy head in one of its co-educational secondary schools. We never doubted that neighbourhood schools, primary and secondary, would be the ones for our children. Our views were the norm in Sheffield; very few local people sent their children to independent schools.

It was a culture shock for us to find that London's maintained schools did not enjoy the same general esteem.

Finding our neighbourhood school was not so easy. In Sheffield most parents were happy to choose the secondary linked with their local primary school, but neither our own local borough nor our neighbouring ILEA had any cohesive linking system. Both preferred to offer a wide parental choice of secondary school. Our house was more or less equidistant from three co-educational comprehensive schools. Two were in our own borough, but I knew that we could choose the third, Hampstead School in Camden, which was part of the Inner London domain. Its head was Ted Field, a man whose liberal views on education were reported in the local press. When my daughter joined the school in 1981, she knew the head as a somewhat remote figure.

I do not know what qualities ILEA and the school governors were looking for when they appointed Tamsyn Imison, but it soon became apparent that she intended to run a tighter, more purposeful ship.

Tamsyn came at a time of unprecedented change in schools, their curriculum, and their management. In the 1980s there were almost as many new education acts as there were years, and almost as many significant reports as there were acts. Reports on the teaching of mathematics and English followed reports on the education of children with special needs and children from ethnic minorities. A new national curriculum was imposed. A new system of school governors was set up, and the secretary of state assumed hundreds of new powers. Between the governors and the secretary of state, in the squeezed middle were scores of emasculated local education authorities and the corpse of the former ILEA, its responsibility for schools transferred to boroughs with no previous experience of administering schools.

Among the many radical innovations under consideration were proposals to link the appraisal of teachers to new systems of performance-related pay. In London more than elsewhere, the heads of secondary schools faced unprecedented difficulties in coping with selective on-off strike action by the members of two major unions. Some teachers refused to write reports because they said this was something they had to do in their own free time. I insisted on having a report on David's mathematics, and to his embarrassment one was written for him alone. Heads had to cope too with more radical students. Ted Field's liberal views had taken shape long before Mohican hair or outré dress, and long before the National Union of School Students engaged many young people, especially in London. It says much for Tamsyn and her senior colleagues that they stuck firmly to the school's comprehensive and liberal values, even though they must have felt sometimes as if they were sitting on a bubbling cauldron's lid. To some of their pupils at the time, the prevailing ethos seemed to be nihilistic.

Thirty years after they first enrolled at Hampstead, our children say one of its great strengths was its social and ethnic diversity: there they learnt to appreciate and value people from every kind of background. Once, at a time when public services were beginning to monitor the ethnic origin of their employees, our daughter was astonished when I asked how many black teachers there were at Hampstead. She had no idea. The pupils might rate their teachers as good, bad, or indifferent, but that assessment of their professional competence was their only criterion. Two decades later, our daughter, now a senior teacher herself, speaks warmly of Hampstead's many inspirational teachers: of English and foreign languages, or history and geography, or mathematics, science, and music.

We were, of course, most interested parents, concerned that our children should do well at school. But we were also rather nervous and reticent parents. Margaret was one of Tamsyn's fellow heads, and I was for some time the education officer in a nearby borough, and then the lead consultant in Tamsyn's own post-ILEA borough. We were perhaps a little too nervous about being thought to be pushy. But I did once feel that a young teacher dismissed a little brusquely my proffered comments about my own child's capabilities.

Though we were happy enough with Hampstead's teaching, its pupils' education was constricted. The lack of playing fields nearby meant that outdoor physical education featured less in our children's school life than it had in ours. More serious was that teachers abandoned many out-of-school activities during the long disputes over teachers' hours and conditions, though Dudley Cohen's almost obsessive commitment ensured that Hampstead's orchestras and choirs continued to enthuse and delight. I was perhaps more confident than our son that in the long run, other influences would outweigh any short-term limitations in what the school was able to provide. Outside school, for example, our children acquired a lifelong interest in gymnastics, swimming, scuba diving, cricket, squash, riding, and many other physical activities.

Like almost every previous generation, we would probably say of our own upbringing that whatever its imperfections, 'it never did us any harm'. Hampstead did much better than that. Moira Young's enthusiastic teaching led our two to read geography at high-ranking universities, a sound basis for further professional qualifications and a lively interest in the world around them, a world where the ability to stay afloat in a diverse, fluid, and open society is the greatest gift. It says much for Tamsyn's leadership that Hampstead was, and remained throughout the 1980s, a microcosmic model of just such a society.

Yvonne Sarch, The Lady Finsberg

Governor 1977–88

We appointed Tamsyn Imison in 1984, when more structured interviews were beginning. Because I was in the public sector running a successful national head-hunting company, I was involved in this appointment. We included role play, which was interesting as some of the candidates refused to participate. The governors were looking for a change from the previous regime. They wanted someone who would be able to cope with the highly political situation of the time, both on the school governing body and with the ILEA. We wanted someone who could eyeball the powers that be and stand up for the school. We also wanted someone strongly committed to equal opportunities, and who was positive towards the increasingly multilingual intake of the school. We wanted someone who would manage and disperse the prevalent drugs culture. The environment was a disgrace, covered in graffiti and litter. It looked as if no one cared. We wanted someone to stop the plateauing of exam results and the stagnant feel in the school.

I was a stroppy Irish woman and a conservative who felt marginalized and always left out of the political caucus meetings, but the appointment of a new head teacher changed things.

The major challenge faced by the head and governors in 1985 was the industrial action and the impact of the militant National Union of Teachers (NUT) both internally and externally, which was highly demotivating. The head teacher was an enigma to the staff because she was an NUT member, but highly professional. Over the first five years there was a radical transformation within the school. This was because the head was able to move into the vacuum left by the withdrawal of the militant staff, and interact directly with parents, governors, students, and those staff eager for positive change. In 1986 many of those out of sympathy with the head's inclusive strategies left the school, which gave her, along with the governors, the chance to appoint many excellent new staff committed to school improvement.

One of the many initiatives begun at that time was work shadowing. I had a young Kurdish girl, who was delightful, shadowing me, and that gave me another insight and more direct connection with the students.

One of the most dramatic improvements I noticed was the bringing of colour into the school. It began with the head teacher's office, which was full of bright colour: I remember a lovely picture of a tree, lots of healthy plants, and children's bright paintings. She had a working table, and people came in and out all the time. It had been a macho boys' club atmosphere, where things were agreed with a nudge and a wink. This was dramatically changed, for example, by the head establishing a finance committee open to all, with clear, agreed criteria for the allocation of money.

All the positions of responsibility bar one had been taken by men in 1984. Even the car park had painted signs for the headmaster, deputy headmaster, and senior headmaster. Tamsyn Imison came in with a whoosh and put in basic structures such as agendas and minutes published on time. Previously my letters got 'lost in the post'. Now we all felt we could contribute to school improvement. Slowly but surely many more women took over, giving a balance across the school that became reflected in the newer intakes. Equal opportunity was seen to be operating in a positive and constructive way. My memory is of the buildings being transformed into somewhere welcoming, clean, light, and airy, and of far greater efficiency.

At governors' meetings we knew what we were doing. The governor who spent his time at governors' meetings reading his briefs left. The noise had ceased. The rules had changed, and Local Management of Schools gave the school far more independence.

I left in 1988 when I felt confident that a new generation of parents, governors, and teachers were prepared to work as a team, and were proud of the school because things were on the up.

Liz Williams

Governor 1987–2004

My first relationship with Hampstead was as a parent, but I got to work much more closely with the school when I became a governor, and then chair of the governors.

Hampstead was the obvious choice for our daughters. It was the nearest school, and our local friends were lining up to send their children there. In the days before Ofsted and league tables, we took account of its academic success, our positive impressions from visiting, and how it stood out against one local alternative at the time, for instance in its library provision. We were keen on a mixed school, ours having been single sex, and my husband happened to be familiar with some of the buildings, as he had attended Haberdashers' Aske's there before Hampstead was founded on the site in 1961. Our elder daughter Megan started in 1982 when Ted Field was head, with Harriet following two years later. Both girls progressed well through school and on to university, and are in touch with many friends they made at Hampstead.

Parental involvement was a popular idea at the time, as the way to help your children do well at school, but it was rarely defined and little researched. I had an interest in education issues from my work, and various family members had been involved in schools in various ways, so becoming involved with the school seemed a natural step. I began by helping with the Parent Teacher Association (PTA), and moved on to be elected as a parent governor in 1987.

Changes to the constitution of governing bodies from legislation in the late 1980s brought a greater role for parent governors, and I was the first parent governor at Hampstead to be elected chair. Tamsyn had been a parent campaigner and CASE [Campaign for State Education] member in Richmond, and was welcoming to me in this role. It felt a privilege to be able to see at close quarters the working of an effective senior management team with a dynamic head teacher. Change was a way of life – some being handed down from government, and some coming as a result of successful funding bids. The aim from any change was always to improve the learning opportunities for Hampstead's young people, and Tamsyn was adept in making the changes fit what she wanted for the school, rather than changing the school to fit new requirements.

From appointments of staff I learnt much about what a good lesson looks like, and how young people's enthusiasm can be encouraged. Interviewing staff is a crash course in understanding the curriculum areas, and it was interesting over the years seeing how young teachers developed and took on responsibilities. Tamsyn always looked for teachers who had potential for further promotion, and preferred not to appoint rather than take the wrong person from a poor field. Through being linked to the learning support department, I got to understand the detailed care and support the school provided for individual children with special needs and behaviour problems. A pupil with Down's syndrome who passed her GCSEs and progressed to higher education was a great example of the department's success. Governors got a chance to see young people in action when representatives of the school council came to governors' meetings. Pupils from different years came once a term. Even the youngest pupils were impressive in holding their own in discussions with the governors, and sometimes even ran the meeting for their item. A question on uniform produced a lively debate – was it fair for teachers to be able to wear short belly-tops when pupils were allowed to wear only long belly-tops? The head wisely concluded that 'appropriate dress' was the best way for the uniform policy to cover the foibles of fashion.

Fairness, respect for the young people, and an infectious sense of fun were all a key part of the Hampstead experience. When Tamsyn and I arrived early for one school fair and found the school gates locked, urgent action was needed so parents could get in. The caretaker lived at the back of the site, and in the days before mobiles, the only way to reach him was to knock on his door. Tamsyn was game to climb over the gate, but I persuaded her that her dignity was more important than mine, so it was my job.

In the late 1980s, Local Management of Schools (LMS) delegated budgets and responsibilities to schools, including premises. I chaired the new finance sub-committee and the site development committee. Funding for the school was a major issue. There were many difficult meetings with Camden, where we pressed Hampstead's case for our fair share, and now and then some extra, when the school's position on the edge of the borough made collaboration with other Camden schools difficult. True to its aim to support the learning of all pupils, the school got over this isolation in an innovative way, for example by turning to a local further education college to provide vocational classes in car maintenance for less academic students.

The poor state of the buildings was a major issue, after years of cuts to maintenance budgets and the changing needs of the school. Much head and governor time was spent chasing money to make improvements and remodel various curriculum areas. The first major development came in the library with the creation of a new IT support area, the start of a site development process. Getting wheelchair accessibility was slow, but has finally been achieved. As a strong believer in the value of good design in creating a productive environment for learning, I was pleased we were able to resist moves towards a private finance initiative (PFI) arrangement.

Throughout my nine years as chair, I worked at the Advisory Centre for Education (ACE), a national advice centre for parents of children in state schools, and I valued helpful advice from colleagues on pastoral questions at school. At the same time I was able to contribute experiences from the school on issues such as exclusion to ACE policy discussions, which were fed back to the Department for Education.

Chairing meetings of the governors' exclusion panel could be challenging, especially when the head's decision was overturned. The school tried hard not to exclude children permanently, and much effort was put into examining difficult incidents, listening to the children and adults involved, and finding ways to help children continue with their learning.

I was lucky as chair to have governor colleagues with a wide range of experience of teaching and many other fields, and parents who felt able to challenge the professionals when they felt things could be improved. I also had a good relationship with the head. We took seriously the annual meeting that was required at the time to be held for parents. Attendance was variable and difficult issues were raised, but it was good that this opportunity for contact was available.

Throughout my involvement at Hampstead, the clear message came through that *all* young people can achieve good things, and success goes much wider than academic achievement. It was a good step forward when results from vocational qualifications were reported alongside GCSEs in national tables. All kinds of initiatives at the school showed how vision, enthusiasm, and care for the children can produce wonderful results. I was pleased to be considered part of the team that helped take the school forward.

Chapter 4
Staff voices

Andrea Berkeley

Teacher 1979–94, including roles in the English department, head of sixth, deputy head 1985–94

Head of Preston Manor High School, Brent 1994–2006.
Currently education director of Teaching Leaders (co-founder);
executive coach

Daughters Xanthe and Zoe attended the school

I have become accustomed to opening *The Guardian Review* or *The Sunday Times* and taking pleasure in reading profiles of contemporary literary giants, poetry reviews, or political commentary written by former students I taught at Hampstead, and to occasionally hearing a voice on Radio 4 familiar from a far-off playground.

When Zadie Smith, one of the most successful authors of our day, said in a recent interview following the publication of her fourth novel set in West Hampstead, Kilburn, and Willesden, 'A lot of my friends from my school have turned out to be writers or painters, and I'm just off to see Adam's exhibition', I reflected on just how lucky I had been as a teacher and how timely the trajectory of my professional development.

It is rare for teachers to know how their students turn out in life. School is a place where generations come and go and teachers stay, then fade away. Young people grow up and rarely look back. It is nearly 20 years since I left Hampstead School and since then as many thousands of students have been my focus. But occasionally teachers are rewarded with glimpses of the fruits of their labours. Recently a few unexpected actual or virtual encounters with former students have brought back memories. As the attainment gap between rich and poor widens, despite rising standards in education, I see I was fortunate to experience at an early stage in my career how comprehensive education and commitment to inclusion can achieve both excellence and equity.

I remember the day Zadie Smith started spelling her name with a 'Z' instead of an 'S' on her English essays, and the last sentence in her UCAS personal statement: 'I want to be the first famous black woman writer'. Zadie was always going to excel. But I also remember the school hall raucously packed one evening to support a rather different kind of black achievement. On stage were the rude boys, the dudes, potential trouble, black potential underachievers – but also, as it turned out, one future Amy Winehouse backing singer, one future dancer with Sadler's Wells and one successful chef. Before the event there had been concern from some staff. Would it get out of hand? Were the words of the blues, soul, and rap 'acceptable'? The teachers who supported the event believed in giving the boys agency to perform 'their own music in their own way'.

The audience, from every year group, was loudly in supportive rapture. Spontaneously, Zadie appeared from the back of the hall and sloped onto the stage. Greeted with some surprise from the band, she took the microphone and began to sing *To the End of the Road* after Boys2Men, the hit hip-hop group of the time. There was no question that she belonged or they belonged – or that they belonged together. No division of geeks and cool kids, high-achieving sixth former and Year 10 at risk of exclusion. That was the Hampstead mix, taken for granted, whatever your academic ability, your background, your aspiration, you were accepted.

It was not always like that for students of African-Caribbean origin or mixed heritage, whatever their ability. A decade before, there were more class divisions and less social integration and acceptance of cultural difference. I joined Hampstead School in 1979 as deputy head of English. It was the best of times and the worst of times in London education. There was no national curriculum, no national SATs, and no Ofsted – although Her Majesty's Inspectorate (HMI) might turn up for the odd inspection. There was no appraisal or performance management for teachers, no development and budgetary planning, and the ILEA made all school financial and admissions decisions through powerful local divisional offices. Even the school's heating was controlled from a central location in Cambridge.

The ILEA was in its heyday, and as a young and enthusiastic English teacher I had access to the most imaginative and innovative resources and professional development opportunities from an inspirational English Centre based in Pimlico. Courses and conferences, even year-long secondments, were plentiful and free of charge to teacher or school. I was in my element.

I could be as creative as I liked and only had to worry about exam syllabuses once students reached the fourth year (Year 10). Many teachers like myself felt the two-tier exam system, O Level and CSE, was socially unjust and educationally unsound. If half the student population felt short-changed, then half one's teaching load was also unfulfilled. Most of us cherished the rewards of a bright O level group against the angst of increasingly disaffected and even hostile CSE groups. Actually, there was a hidden third tier – really disruptive and anti-education students and probably those with a special educational need, although I was largely unaware of what that meant at the time – who were banished to off-site alternative provision. One never quite knew what happened to them after that. Very occasionally, one would live in fear of someone suggesting how important it was for one of them to 'return to English for just one lesson' and felt relief when they didn't.

I loved the intellectual stimulation of teaching poetry to small A level groups, then comprising mainly the children of the Hampstead intelligentsia who put their faith in the comprehensive ideal.

I welcomed the advent of the GCSE. I can visualize my last O level class vividly, mainly because it was during the punk era, and as Hampstead had no school uniform, the class contained a Mohican and several multi-coloured spiky haircuts. I can see Sadie Frost, now a well-known actress and designer, at the back on a table, cross-legged in fishnet stockings and a biker jacket, next to a future bricklayer, a soon-to-be teenage mother, and a future theatre director.

So it was the best of times for ambitious teachers, loving their subjects and wanting to be creative. But there was no accountability, and although opportunities existed, professional development was largely self-directed. Sixty per cent left school at 16 without adequate qualifications, and 20 per cent of those who progressed to post-16 education were ungraded at A level.

As the catchment area began to change, the intake became more diverse and inequalities started to show, in poorer attainment and disaffection and disruptive behaviour, particularly marked among students from black and ethnic minority backgrounds. So the joyful 1993 R&B and soul evening that was to pack the school hall with such a diverse range of students in years to come could not have taken place then. Those were the days when staff complained of groups of black students 'intimidating' them by gathering on the staircase near the staffroom, and when O level classes were predominantly white and CSE classes comprised mainly ethnic minority students. That was when there were no black students in the sixth form, and when black parents decided to confront educational failure by demanding a parents' group.

The changing school intake and the conflicting demands of parents of children with varying needs became increasingly challenging, exacerbated by the teaching unions' industrial action in the early 1980s that took the form of a work to rule, which resulted in deterioration of student motivation and behaviour. Anyone who disagreed was subjected to bullying tactics from the extreme branches of the teaching unions. In the end, teaching itself became more of a daily challenge as students, particularly the most needy, became demoralized in the wake of examination reform and the introduction of the GCSE. At the time I was completing postgraduate study on language and reading development with the Open University, and facing the challenge of addressing the increasing literacy needs of the school's changing intake.

In this climate a new head arrived to provide the vision, direction, and aspiration that the school needed during a time of rapid demographic change, and at the advent of unprecedented systemic educational reform. Tamsyn's arrival was timely. Wholly committed to the comprehensive ideal and what we would now call 'inclusion', she had the skills, the political and emotional intelligence, and the creative – some would say Machiavellian – strategic thinking to drive the change that was needed.

Flipping forward to 2012, a chance encounter brought me back to the cusp of change – the testing but exhilarating first years of Tamsyn's leadership, and how that made a difference to so many people's lives. Earlier this year I accompanied my daughter to a wedding reception where she was assembling the cake. Zoe, a former Hampstead student herself, owns a bake shop and tea room. I was just keeping her company and did not expect to meet anyone I knew. As we walked in, a group of middle-aged, predominantly black men chatting near the doorway stopped their conversations and one called out 'Mrs Berkeley!' Now in their 40s, smartly dressed, eager to introduce their wives and show photographs of their children, these men were from my CSE class of 1984, one of the first of the less academic groups to benefit from curriculum innovations and change in ethos. After the initial shock of recognition, their faces began to look to me exactly as they had then. Gallantly, they also said, 'You look the same, Miss!' – except that I meant it.

I can see them now, and how their good-humoured rowdiness may have been misperceived and led to exclusion in another school context. It was striking that they all spoke fondly of their time at school, grateful for the opportunities they had received, and the bond of friendship they had maintained over time. Jokes and anecdotes flowed to illustrate the affection and gratitude they felt. I admit to a little surprise, as I don't think we were ready then to give them the education they deserved. But perhaps they knew we cared. I certainly remember many a heartfelt discussion about them as individuals with their tutors. They had all done pretty well for themselves in life. Perhaps they hadn't gone to university – although two did take degrees later in life – but they had succeeded in business or trade and were contented with their lives. Perhaps we did more for them than we thought. And, just like my own daughters, they are all still in contact with their friends from school. Perhaps social media today helps in this respect, but I think it's more than that. I observe this social ease with my daughters, the ability to mix and communicate with people from different backgrounds, is indeed the result of social change. But the contribution of comprehensive education to this very social change is rarely recognized.

Hearing these students' life stories reminded me of an anecdote in Guy Claxton's *What's the Point of School?* What we think we are teaching or offering young people may well be at odds with what they are actually taking away. Many of them were considered ne'er-do-wells at the time, but in reality, although they may have been resisting education and pushing every boundary – what teenager doesn't or shouldn't? – they successfully took the nurturing they had received into their adult lives. To live a successful life is not always measured out in examination results.

Tamsyn's arrival marked the beginning of professional enlightenment for me – and I believe for the school. I wanted to make a difference but felt cautious about seeking promotion while bringing up a young family. There were few female role models at that time – and I suspect they are diminishing as I write in the new macho world of hero headship – and Tamsyn provided the most powerful one for me. Without holding a significant management post, it was difficult to influence. There was a great deal of resistance to change among staff, so Tamsyn needed allies, a critical mass of teachers like me who embraced her philosophy of distributed leadership.

Following English department management, Tamsyn gave me opportunities to hold acting posts as examinations officer, deputy head of year, then head of sixth form, until 1986, when I was appointed deputy head with responsibility for CPD and post-16 (later 14–19) education. When nine years later I was challenged about staying so long in one school – 15 years in total – at my interview for headship, I was able to cite all the different whole-school initiatives and innovations I had led during that time of rapid education reform. I can't think of a year in which there was not an opportunity to lead on something exciting and new. In fact, at one point I was nicknamed 'deputy head in charge of government initiatives'. I'm not too sure about the accuracy of that one, as I thought I was principally engaged in subverting or, as we called it, 'domesticating' government initiatives.

That chance meeting with a group of former students brought back to me how important those initiatives were in making Hampstead a more inclusive school. We could have done so much more for them had they attended the school a few years later. The school was only just beginning to change.

I was still enjoying teaching John Milton's *Paradise Lost* to my A level classes and was delighted when in one year, 12 of them were accepted at Oxford or Cambridge, but I was becoming increasingly convinced that we needed to broaden curriculum provision for less academically inclined students and to forge more links with business and industry.

Although now commonplace in schools, in the 1980s it was considered quite revolutionary to arrange work experience placements for all sixth formers and to explore giving parity of esteem to vocational as well as academic qualifications. So Hampstead was at the forefront of broadening the scope of careers education and links with industry, which led to my secondment to the Department of Trade and Industry (DTI). This opportunity opened many doors and provided me and other key staff with the knowledge and understanding – and contacts with external agencies – to successfully bid for one of the first Technology School Initiatives (or whatever it was called then!). This gave us the start-up funding to begin integrating new technologies, not just in science and technology departments but across the curriculum.

Another unexpected encounter highlighted how much we underestimate the impact of those new technologies. Out of the blue I received a long letter from a former O level student. She had tracked me down, predicting that I might still be in the education system. Lucy Yeoman's touching letter recalled English lessons she remembered 25 years later, when she decided to abandon her BBC career to train as a teacher. She had completed her probationary year and marvelled at how we had all been able to prepare lessons without the internet, without computers, without video, without even a photocopier. Yes indeed, how did we do that?

It was refreshing that no idea was too crazy for Tamsyn, as long as one could argue the benefit for the students – all students – and have a strategy for getting staff on board. She was prepared to take the risk. One had to convince other members of the senior team of course. Many examples come to mind. For instance, on returning from my DTI secondment I was convinced that all sixth form students should have experience of vocational as well as academic education, including qualifications with parity of esteem if not progression currency (that would come next, I hoped). So a range of compulsory General National Vocational Qualifications (GNVQs) was offered to A level as well as vocational students. It didn't last, of course, and even today, when vocational courses have more recognition and status, the same academic/vocational divide remains. However, I was allowed to give it a try, and there was a germ of an idea there – and I'm still smiling from hearing Ed Miliband subscribe to a similar idea and propose such a scheme in his 2012 Labour Party conference speech.

When I suggested counterbalancing and accompanying this initiative with a very intellectually challenging *History of Ideas* course instead of the usual sixth form induction, I was given the backing, the resources, and a whole week to play with. To my astonishment, academic luminaries like professors Martin Kemp and Steve Jones, economist John Ashworth, historian David Starkey, and politicians and leading figures in the arts world accepted invitations to speak, and the whole sixth form team and representatives from every academic department set about devising schemes of work covering the history of ideas from Ancient Greece and Rome to the present day. I still have a photograph of that planning team of staff on my study wall.

Many happy moments remain – some too funny or risqué to put on paper, as Tamsyn does have a wicked sense of humour. But mostly what I took from Hampstead to my own headship was how much I had learnt about leadership and management. I wrote a *Memo to myself* before I left, some structured reflection on what I had learnt from Tamsyn and her senior leadership team, and here it is:

Memo to myself

LEADERSHIP FOR LEARNING – LESSONS FROM HAMPSTEAD

- Have a vision, set direction, and plan strategically
- Be child-centred, focus on individual needs – consider the whole child
- Use performance data analysis and target setting to raise attainment
- Have a clear focus on teaching and learning, especially literacy
- Embed systematic processes for monitoring and evaluation
- Invest in staff recruitment and retention – teachers are your most precious asset – and in engaging CPD
- Tackle weak teaching with targeted support
- Create a culture for learning for both students and staff – think consciously about ethos and branding
- Banish cynicism and complacency and replace with a 'no excuses' and 'success for all' culture
- Conceptualize the organization and clarify roles, responsibilities, accountability
- Make clear who is making decisions but always consult
- Always be explicit about reasons for decisions/changes
- Delegate completely, but steer and support – empower people but hold them accountable

- Keep meetings to a minimum and focus on core business – no staff meetings, only briefings
- Have a development plan and cycle of self-review – and training priorities and plan

TALENT

- Spot it, invest in it, treasure it
- When talent spotted, find ways of developing it and support
- Grow the next layer of leadership
- Succession plan
- Develop middle leaders – where the action is
- Empower them, raise their profile, praise them

BUILD TEAMS

- Train them, trust them, free them, praise them
- Give them autonomy but monitor and support
- Measure performance
- Balance of pressure and support
- Grasp the nettle of weak teaching
- Pupil tracking and target setting
- Needs-led curriculum and literacy strategy
- Social inclusion and behaviour management
- Provide equality by recognizing difference
- Consider the emotional factors in teaching and learning and have emotionally intelligent approaches to disaffection

ETHOS AND CULTURE

- Embed core values in the learning environment
- Make school memorable – collective celebration, pride, praise
- Take risks
- Pay attention to the 'little things'
- Study success, start with it, communicate it
- Move from strengths, manage weaknesses
- Focus on excellence and celebrate it
- Banish cynicism and complacency
- Praise openly, genuinely, frequently
- Have high expectations always, communicate them and live them myself

Deirdre Broadbent

Teacher 1995–2003, head of music

Assistant head teacher and head of music, St Cecilia's School, 2003–05. Currently mentor for PGCE students at the Institute of Education

I had taught A level music to Hampstead sixth formers in Camden School for Girls and knew the school for six years before my appointment in 1995. Music was at a low ebb then, with around eight pupils at GCSE and no A level. The department had been run by a talented, newly qualified teacher (NQT) for nearly a year. Choral work had been good, but attendance was compulsory if students learnt an instrument in school, which resulted in some reluctant students. There was a wind band, but no orchestra, scanty resources, only one teaching room, with the stage in the school hall doubling as a classroom. The few peripatetic instrumental teachers on local authority contracts seemed to have no pupils and to sit about reading. We were delighted when we were allotted more practice rooms, a second teaching room, and a recording studio. Suddenly we had an airy, properly equipped department where pupils would hang out at break and lunchtime.

Work in Key Stage 3 (KS3) was the main focus in driving up standards and increasing the joy experienced by pupils in their music lessons. We mainly achieved this by freeing children up, taking risks, giving them less chalk and talk, and allowing them more responsibility for their own learning. Moving the curriculum away from relying on one type of music to a wider overview, including world music, jazz, pop, and folk made a huge difference to the learning. To do so we invested in many more classroom instruments, including African and Indian drums, a sitar, and other tuned instruments such as xylophones and metallophones. The head was totally supportive of this extra funding, making the department come alive again. All aspects of the music syllabus would be taught through pupils making music and learning to listen respectfully to each other. Assessment would be made on the spot, every lesson, according to key stage guidelines. Pupils would have feedback on a regular basis to inform them of their progress.

After one year of the new KS3 curriculum, 27 very mixed-ability pupils chose the subject for GCSE, causing timetabling chaos at first. The nature of the KS4 intake changed dramatically, with pupils who had never learnt to play an instrument or had abandoned it after primary school, together with others at grade 7 or 8 in performing ability. I have always reckoned that differentiation in music is wider than in any other subject, and the challenge was to create a supportive and respectful atmosphere in this group. The school and governors were immediately responsive, and every music GCSE student was allowed free one-to-one instrumental teaching to raise their opportunity for success in Year 11. With a new and vibrant peripatetic instrumental team, pupils came on at a terrific pace. Some were performing music from the grade 4 syllabus very ably by the time they came to perform for their final exam, after learning an instrument for only five terms.

Musical literacy was an issue, especially when writing down their musical ideas. Those who hadn't learnt an instrument hadn't learnt to read or write music. They had been taught the basic rules of writing rhythms and pitch, but if you don't have to use this information on a daily basis, it never becomes the speedy second nature it needs to be. For some pupils with learning difficulties, it was another difficult new language. So it became essential to develop a system to help these pupils find a way of putting their ideas on paper. Working with one boy who had extremely poor literacy helped me devise a simple but effective way of writing down music. More information about this can be found in my articles (Broadbent, 2008; 2009a; 2009b).

A level development

When I was appointed, a main focus was to prevent leakage of talented musicians to neighbouring schools after GCSE. Six of the seven GCSE students I took over who took the exam in 1996 wanted to continue their music studies to A level. I kept four who completed A level music at Hampstead with good grades, one gaining a choral scholarship to Magdalene College, Oxford. We never lost another A level music student after that year, and the subject continued to grow and have extremely good outcomes. Several alumni are solo performers, and many have become music teachers.

Our extended and refurbished music space could now house the new development of Music Technology A level. With expert staff appointed, I still taught on the course to keep my eye on the ball. Finally, we started a Performing Arts A level with the drama and dance departments, which filled in an important space in the curriculum. After six years there were now 100 students studying music at Hampstead at Key Stages 4 and 5, from only eight before I arrived.

Enthusing students

Encouraging youngsters' instrumental lessons at school is a foundation of a successful department. Soon we had a teacher for every instrument, and some had two. Three hundred children were now learning an instrument. There was a big demand for electric guitar and drum kit lessons, and this led to introducing a Bands' Night so our pupils could show their talents. But there was still a gap, as many very musical pupils came from the club music scene and were not interested in acoustic instruments. This was successfully filled by a group called Bigga Fish, who came into school and taught the current craze, DJing. They taught on Mondays, and a new type of student arrived in the department, the kind who had so far been difficult to reach. Some, almost all boys, had not been in school on Monday mornings for weeks and were now showing up, and on time. This helped to sustain good behaviour, as any infringements of the school rules were reported to me and lessons stopped until an improvement was shown.

Music making across the school

At the start of the 1995 school year there was only a jazz band, started by my colleague. Beginning with a junior choir and a junior training orchestra, we gradually built up the senior choir, orchestra, and wind band. An organized music tour of Belgium in summer 1997 helped to motivate students – and did they come out of the woodwork! We continued the initiative, taking the music ensembles away for a week every other year. Having the students with us all day, we could focus on our standard of performance, rehearse for longer and more intensively, and greatly improve by doing the same concert several times in different venues. Soon we had a perfectly decent little orchestra, a training orchestra for beginners, a wind band and a choir, and of course, our jazz band. Each September I re-auditioned every player in the orchestras, moving juniors up into chamber orchestra, giving other talented players leadership positions, and generally having very high expectations from all players. Peripatetic staff helped.

Performing in competitions was also good for the students – they had to play or sing their very best, and heard other groups against which to measure their standard. For example, an *a cappella* chamber choir performed in the Queen Elizabeth Hall in the finalists' concert of the Music for Youth Competition. Gradually, extra-curricular groups became more and more able, and the orchestra played many standard repertoire pieces. Schubert's *Unfinished Symphony*, Beethoven's *Leonora Overture*, Bach's 4th *Brandenburg Concerto*, Haydn's *Cello Concerto*, and Mozart's *Eine Kleine Nachtmusik* stand out. Each year we either toured in the summer or staged musicals, starting with *Bugsy Malone*, then *Joseph and the Amazing Technicolor Dreamcoat*, *The Wiz*, *West Side Story*, and *Grease*. I was most proud of the fact that in my last year at Hampstead, we put on Purcell's opera *Dido and Aeneas*, with our own students in the cast and a chorus of students, parents, and staff.

Hampstead School developed a total community of music makers during my time there, with students, parents, teaching and other staff able to participate in a variety of challenging and exciting musical activities. We had a Hampstead choral society – students, caretakers, secretarial and teaching staff, and parents and friends of the school. With the school orchestra and chamber orchestra we performed Vivaldi's *Gloria*, Handel's *Messiah*, Bach's *Magnificat,* and Mozart's *Requiem.* All the soloists were students.

I loved the fact that Hampstead was a true comprehensive with students from every kind of background, from the estates around the school, to pupils from middle-class families in Hampstead and West Hampstead, and everything in between. We had students from all over the world, some of whom brought their own culture vividly to the classroom. I remember one child from a traveller community performing a fire-eating act in a GCSE music concert. (Health and Safety would have been appalled.) I valued this non-selective education. All children have equal importance and need the same opportunities to discover their potential. Creating a homogeneous community in school, where all kinds of students mix, cooperate, and learn, leads to a better hope for our greater society.

Since leaving the school I have worked as an assistant head teacher, lectured and tutored at the Institute of Education, University of London, and undertaken consultancy and journalism. At Hampstead I witnessed that there is little you cannot do, given proper encouragement and support. You just need to maintain your vision of excellence, keep your energy levels high, and stay healthy.

Anney Bulbeck

Teacher 1985–8, craft design and technology department (CDT)

Currently teaching; has run own design company

I first knew Hampstead School as a newly qualified teacher in September 1985. I was excited and a little nervous at the prospect of working in one of the ILEA's flagship schools. Hampstead's excellent reputation was well known. I was also excited by the challenge of being the first woman CDT teacher at the school, with a personal mission to make what was then still a boys' subject girl-friendly.

The first class I taught was an all-boys fifth year (Year 11) woodwork group. At the time, teaching woodwork to 20 or more 16-year-old boys seemed a daunting prospect. They were described as challenging, but I was also told they had poor attendance. Word soon got out that their new woodwork teacher was a woman, and of course they all turned up to check me out. Attendance was 100 per cent! I am only just over 5 feet tall and looked quite young back in 1985. The novelty soon wore off, and over the course of that first term, they learnt to respect me and appreciate my woodworking skills. I would reproach them for asking for 'tree wood'. The head teacher was a great support to me during that first term and would regularly visit my workshop during lessons. This was my only all-boys group because, to my delight, and with the appointment of a second female teacher, girls started opting in numbers for the subject.

The excellent ILEA Design and Technology Centre ran many innovative courses for teachers across London, from which I benefited considerably. It widened and developed my CDT skills, which I then brought back into school: for example, designing with electronics. This led to exciting curriculum developments that inspired many girls and challenged boys to tackle design problems successfully. I met other female CDT teachers at the centre, and swapped notes on what we were doing to make our subject interesting and relevant to girls.

I remember in those early days Tamsyn invited me to a debate at the House of Commons on the subject of girls' achievement in single-sex and co-educational schools. A group of our sixth form girls was to debate with girls from a local private all-girls school. I remember our girls looking about the place – all those statues and the imposing décor – but they didn't seem intimidated. Austin Mitchell MP chaired, and our girls argued that a truly comprehensive co-educational school was the ideal, because it most fully equips girls to achieve their best in both higher education and the world of work. Against this was the argument that girls always do better in all-girls' schools because they are not distracted or put down by the boys. I believe our girls won the argument in the end.

Looking back, the real challenge in my first year was in my tutor group. I had sole responsibility for a group of 30 lively 11-year-olds. It felt like a privilege, and it was amazing to see how their individual personalities developed throughout that first year. During the summer term, something happened that I will never forget: the death of a member of the group, and how we all dealt with it. It was a beautiful sunny day, and when I did the register in the morning, I noticed that one boy was absent. In the last lesson I was summoned to a deputy head's office and told that the boy had been killed in a car accident while returning from a dental appointment with his mother. I could hardly take it in. I was asked what I wanted to do. Instinctively, I knew that I had to tell the tutor group myself and immediately, so that the force of this shocking and devastating news would impact on us all at the same time.

The tutor group was let out of their lesson early. They filed into the form room, uncharacteristically silent. I have no idea now what exactly I said, but I told them without crying myself. Then I did find myself getting tearful. Most of them stayed, and we talked and grieved together for a while. He was a happy, delightful, bright boy with a wide circle of friends within the tutor group.

I attended the funeral at Golders Green cemetery a week later with tutor group members who had been at primary school with him. I remember it was another beautiful summer's day and feeling it was a duty that I didn't want to fulfil, because I might fall apart in front of those children. They were such a great support, as it turned out. One girl remembered to bring a big box of tissues, which we passed up and down the pew. My heart went out to his poor mother.

I realize now that I had learnt the craft of being an effective tutor by the end of my first year. This was only possible because of the support, trust, and respect given to me by Hampstead School. In turn, I gave my tutor group support, trust, and respect. This ethos pervaded the whole school. Everyone was valued and respected as a unique individual. I have met many teachers since who resent the extra responsibility of being a form tutor. At Hampstead it was an integral and highly valued part of the job: the education of the whole child. I stayed with my tutor group until I left Hampstead in 1988, when they were at the end of their third year, and I have many happy memories.

Hampstead was one of several outstanding London comprehensives with no school uniform. Why would a school that respects and trusts every individual student need or want one? Students were able to express themselves, their personal tastes and styles in what they wore, and also learn appropriate dress codes that showed respect for others. The overwhelming majority respected this freedom and did not abuse it. It allowed the social and cultural diversity of the school to bloom and be celebrated.

The senior management team was always fully involved in the whole life of the school and this was very important. At break times I expected to see Tamsyn, the head teacher, in the playground talking to students and helping staff with break duties. She was a visible presence around the school and led an effective hands-on team, a contrast with today's aloof, invisible school managers.

I returned to teach design and technology part-time at Hampstead in early 1990 for a year. Going back was easy. It felt like returning to my family. I had kept in touch with colleagues in the school, and over those years made many enduring friendships. I believe this was because staff felt we really were all in it together, a collegiate group, doing our very best for the students and the school.

At Hampstead teaching and learning were central to the life of the school, led by an understanding of the importance of every individual. Having recently returned to teaching, I notice the contrast and am now painfully aware that many schools seem dominated by targets and petty rules and an enormous increase in paperwork.

I have taken many things from my experience of working at Hampstead School. But above all I learnt that if people are trusted, truly valued, and respected, they will perform to the best of their ability. This is true for both teachers and students. Hampstead showed me the best of comprehensive education, a truly diverse social and cultural mix that achieved excellence through respect for the whole community and high expectations. I am convinced that good comprehensive schools are essential for the future of our society, democracy, equality, and social progress.

Olly Button

Teacher 1999–2004

Currently principal, Queensbury Academy, Dunstable

Mixed, multicultural, 11–18, inclusive yet academically focused, creative and forward looking, developing next practice in teaching and learning, high profile and offering good opportunities for career development. Such was my list of requirements when searching for my first promoted position after two years as a main-scale mathematics teacher learning the basic tools of my trade. When I saw the advert for deputy head of mathematics in the *Times Educational Supplement* in October 1998, Hampstead School appeared to meet all of these requirements, so I submitted my application.

Despite losing out to an internal candidate for the second in maths job, the students and staff to whom I taught my demonstration lesson responded positively, and I was offered, and accepted without hesitation, the role of Key Stage 3 maths co-ordinator. I was later promoted to deputy head of maths and finally to head of the mathematics faculty, a role I enjoyed immensely. My interactions with the mathematics team at the local authority School Improvement Service gave me the opportunity to be named as one of two leading maths teachers for the London Borough of Camden. Similar to an advanced skills teacher, but without any additional remuneration, this entailed teaching demonstration lessons to visitors from other schools in the borough.

My vision as head of maths was simple: to develop an outstanding mathematics faculty based on a relentless focus on excellent teaching with a mutually supportive team ethos. Clearly this vision was closely aligned to that of the whole school and its credo of *Learning Together, Achieving Together*, a sentiment in which I had always believed. Being relatively near the start of my career, I saw challenges rather than barriers to achieving this vision. Perhaps the most significant concerned the low expectations of many students in terms of their own potential and achievement. Unsurprisingly, this was more prevalent among the students from deprived backgrounds. It contrasted sharply with the self-assuredness of most of the small number of middle-class students from West Hampstead to be found in many classes. This contrast was one of the idiosyncrasies of Hampstead School which, when managed effectively by the staff, was a key to the overall success and ethos of the school.

As with most schools with challenging intakes, the low literacy levels of some on entry, particularly some white working-class students and students with English as an additional language, put extra demands on the skills of the teacher to plan and deliver lessons that were both accessible and challenging to all. Effective personalization was essential for teaching to be engaging and enjoyable, and for the diverse range of students to make good progress. In turn this signalled the importance of continuously developing staff and maintaining a sharp focus on improving pedagogy, both at departmental and whole-school level. The need for a high level of skill among teachers, combined with a shortage of good applicants in subjects such as mathematics, emphasized the need for a 'grow your own' approach to developing talent. Hampstead School had clearly embraced this idea, and it served the mathematics faculty well.

As head of faculty, I was careful to encourage post holders to lead items on our departmental meeting agenda. I also encouraged other members of the team to develop innovative and engaging ways of teaching mathematical concepts. In the faculty room we talked frequently about maths and teaching. We readily shared ideas and resources, and paired up with other teachers to jointly plan and team-teach particular topics. There was always a good synergy among the team and an enjoyable buzz that made it feel more like entertainment than work. This I believe was key to our success, and something I have yet to succeed in recreating on a larger scale.

Working within these guiding principles to achieve a vision aligned to that of the whole school, we transformed the mathematics faculty into an outstanding department that became one of relatively few nationally to achieve Lead Department status under the Excellence in Cities initiative.

Although we had always worked well as a team, this recognition galvanized us further, providing the momentum for continued improvements. It also helped to ensure effective succession planning. The team had become greater than the sum of its parts, and consequently was not significantly affected when key team members inevitably left to take up promoted positions elsewhere.

Some months later, I was asked to lead whole-school training focused on improving teaching and leading a high-performing department. This was both rewarding and great for my own personal development, and it proved to be a defining moment in my own career. On reflection, the skilful leadership of the head teacher both recognized and disseminated good practice across the school as a whole, achieved an enormous amount of buy-in, and significantly developed me as an individual middle leader. I remember thinking at the time that I must remember the power of such a mutually beneficial, albeit simple, distributed leadership strategy.

From the first day I visited Hampstead School to the day I left, I particularly enjoyed the vibrant and exciting atmosphere created by such a diverse community of students. Hampstead School had a buzz about it, which meant that teachers enjoyed teaching and students for the most part enjoyed learning. The head teacher and senior staff of the school had managed to create a culture of earned autonomy and intelligently distributed leadership that was empowering and strongly motivational. Staff achievements were recognized and praised, which set the tone for teachers' interactions with all the students they came into contact with. There was a mutually supportive ethos among staff within and across different curriculum areas, and a strong commitment to teamwork. The sense of contributing to something important – something beyond one's own classroom – of making a difference and being recognized for doing so, was hugely gratifying, and meant that morale among staff was high and the atmosphere usually buoyant.

During my time at Hampstead School, we saw year-on-year improvements in the proportion of students achieving at least five good grades at GCSE, alongside improvements in behaviour and attitudes to learning. Unsurprisingly, these improvements coincided with a steady increase in the quality of teaching across the school and improvements in consistency within and across different areas of the curriculum. Perhaps more surprising is that these improvements happened against the backdrop of increasing deprivation. Hampstead School had more students from the estates of Willesden and Harlesden and fewer privileged middle-class students from more affluent areas. The school had nonetheless developed a very strong climate of learning and achievement as well as an excellent reputation in the borough and beyond, and so appeared unaffected by the change in its intake.

The recognition I had gained from achieving lead department status and my role as a leading maths teacher helped me to achieve my first promotion to senior leadership as assistant head teacher at Villiers High School in Southall in April 2004. I was fortunate to develop and implement a 'learning to learn' curriculum, work with many leading thinkers on the subject of teaching and learning, and co-author a book (Strang *et al.*, 2006). In 2006, I became deputy head at Albany School in Enfield, and since May 2012 have been principal for the new Queensbury Academy in Dunstable, Bedfordshire.

The five years I spent at Hampstead School cemented my belief in the power of the comprehensive school model. I witnessed first-hand the importance of distributing leadership: the rapid improvements generated by empowering staff, nurturing their talents, and playing to individual strengths. Creating such an ethos among the staff in the school transferred almost subconsciously to the relationships between teachers and their students. The students enjoyed learning and developing because their teachers modelled this on a daily basis. The head teacher used to say: 'We are all mirrors'. With hindsight I can see what she meant.

Clearly, one of the most important achievements of the head teacher and senior staff of the school was to continually emphasize that good teachers in a challenging urban comprehensive could easily be outstanding teachers in a school with a more privileged intake. Teachers at Hampstead were not the poor relations of those from the many high-profile, fee-paying independent schools in the surrounding area – quite the opposite. This rightly engendered a sense of pride and enjoyment among staff that again was reflected onto the students. Schools like Hampstead are where education matters most.

My experience at Hampstead School instilled an unshakeable conviction that inclusion and achievement are not mutually exclusive. Using effective personalization within the curriculum and the classroom, the best schools can – and do – embrace diversity and create an environment where all our students, regardless of their background or prior attainment, can achieve success.

With visionary and intelligently distributed leadership, together with relentless commitment and energy, these schools transform the lives of the individual students and staff who learn and grow in them, and the communities they serve. Our challenge is to spread this message as widely as possible.

Heather Daulphin

Teacher 1992–present, head of history 1992–7; head of sixth 1997–9.

Currently deputy head teacher; leadership development coach with Teaching Leaders (2010–12); education consultant to Achievement for All, supporting vulnerable learners (2012–present).

In my position as a leader of pedagogy and the curriculum, I could see we were renowned both locally and nationally for being both creative and innovative. The climate at Hampstead in the 1990s made it safe for people to take risks, provided these led to staff and student learning and achievement. It is also true that governors, led by the head teacher, were skilled at appointing highly talented risk-takers who aspired to develop learning. I felt I was given permission to be myself and not fit a mould established by the school. This led to a high-energy community of motivated, creative lead learners whose contributions to the whole school spilled out into many significant extra-curricular activities such as the Model United Nations (MUN) and debating under Donal O'Hagan; the many joint creative projects from the National Playwright Commissioning initiative; joint staff and student visits abroad; politics, and in particular, developing the student voice.

We were one of the first schools to embrace students' evaluation of teachers, and to include students in the selection of staff, which I experienced when I was head of sixth and deputy head. The school council was recognized as an important contributor to school policy, and its reports to governors were taken very seriously.

Learning Together, Achieving Together as a principle was built into the way the school operated. As one of the first schools to undergo the Investors in People process in 1995, we found that a high proportion of staff participated in professional development. We had our own in-house Master's programme run by the Institute of Education, like our initial teacher inset that involved the whole staff as well as the 12 taking their Master's. Many like me were already following Master's courses at the Institute of Education and elsewhere. Others took on advanced counselling courses at the Tavistock Clinic. It was expected that many staff would contribute to our in-house training. Our approach to performance management was both constructive and rigorous. We were well ahead on monitoring and evaluation, with action taken to improve teaching and learning. There was a climate of praise and recognition by the school community, and by the many high-profile national figures regularly invited into school. This also led to colleagues being invited to contribute to many national working parties and think tanks. I was on the

National Citizenship Committee. Tamsyn was on the National Committee on Creativity and Cultural Education.

One of the successes for me was developing a broader, more inclusive programme for our sixth form, leading to further and higher education. By integrating more vocational courses alongside the traditional A levels, we raised the aspirations and achievement for many more students. We developed a compact with the nearby University of North London, which also widened our student participation rate. The quality of vocational work prominently displayed in the sixth form opened many people's eyes to the value and rigour of such courses. It is no accident that so many of our students have been highly successful and have gone on to be leaders.

We embraced new technologies across the whole curriculum and in my area – history – we used many different techniques, such as cut and paste, sorting, classifying, and assisting with writing. Making newspapers was a particularly good strategy for boys, who found extended writing more taxing than did our girls. Andrea Smith and I gave joint inset training to local schools and others.

Former Education Secretary Estelle Morris said, 'No excuses, only explanations', and that has always stuck with me. Our approach was to find ways of engaging every young person in learning, and never giving up. We expected every student to be capable of more. We engaged in whole-school scrutinies of pupils' workbooks, and used our findings to improve on our practice.

I am the successful product of a local comprehensive school, and there is no doubt that with non-selective schools, the mixing of aspirational students with other students raises the aspirations of all and allows social mobility. Such schools force teachers to find ways of addressing all learning needs across the whole spectrum of attainment, and we find in such schools that every child can achieve.

Athy Demetriades

Teacher 1986–98

Currently head teacher, Northgate School, Barnet
At Hampstead I was on a steep learning curve. I gained the skills to be the teacher I aspired to be, learnt the meaning of camaraderie by working with amazing staff teams, and experienced a true sense of belonging. We had real fun.

I was first appointed as second in charge of English as an additional language (EAL), arriving full of hope to pursue my belief in equality and inclusion, with many impossible dreams and a certain degree of fear as a young teacher. As a specialist physical education (PE) teacher, my first challenge was competence in my second specialism. The local education authority's training supported this. The challenges of teaching English with over 60 different languages represented were enormous. We were a small team coping with requests for skilled support from every department, and from students with a need and thirst to learn English. I also became a tutor for the first time.

Before the end of my first year, with the encouragement of Andrea Berkeley, a deputy head, I became head of Year 8 and thoroughly enjoyed this job, which I did for 10 years. It was made clear that I would be responsible for the academic, personal, and emotional progress of every student and the year 8 tutor group leaders. Leading and managing a team, alongside managing the most delightful but challenging year group, was a turning point in my career. I began setting myself, my team, and most importantly my students the highest learning and achievement targets.

Our expectations for GCSE for this Year 8 group were for 60 per cent A–C grades – the national average was 40 per cent. Nothing less was good enough, but along the way students needed to enjoy their learning. Parents became part of my team, and we organized barn dances, international evenings, weekly tutor group assemblies, study weekends, and regular activity holidays. The students met and exceeded their targets in Year 11 with an astounding 68 per cent A–C grades. This confirmed that the key was to set high expectations for all, including myself, and to lead and manage my team so that we could motivate and inspire our students to achieve their best. It was a steep learning curve. I learnt to become solution-focused, as going to the head teacher with any challenge resulted in one of two outcomes. I would either be given educational books to read and review, or be asked for my solution. I soon learnt never to go with any problems until I was prepared and could say, 'Here is the challenge that I face and these are my possible responses to it'. However, I also knew that if I was unable to work towards a solution, support and guidance were always there.

The next year's group exceeded their targets, as did I. With the encouragement of the students in my year group, I completed my Master's degree. They also persuaded, supported, and guided me alongside the head teacher to fight for the rights of refugee students, our 'invisible students'. At the time the divisive system of teaching English as a Second Language (ESL) under Section 11 of the Local Government Act (1966) made funds available 'to help meet the special needs of a significant number of people of commonwealth origin with language or customs that differ from the rest of the community'. This meant that we could only be available to those second-language learners from the British Commonwealth. However, the department was determined to teach and support all of the 50 per cent of the school roll still at early stages of English-language acquisition. We developed a peer partnership programme, training self-selected students in the year group in supporting their peers. With equal weighting given to both partners, the benefits were wide for both those who were trained and those recently arrived who needed language and emotional support. Soon sixth form students also supported their peers in classes.

From 1989, when the plight of refugee students was immense, Hampstead School became the driving force behind many local, national, and global initiatives. In 1991 we had 120 refugee children: vulnerable, often unaccompanied minors who had recently arrived without any support. Some slept rough in adult men's shelters, others boarded with families who spoke their language but had very restricted accommodation. None were entitled to free school meals.

A Year 9 student arrived at the school from Somalia. She was unable to communicate in English. As her head of year, I spoke to her tutor group about how they could include and support her, but a simple game of 'nudge' with her peers led to our student having a panic attack, in which she stopped breathing for a short while. Being an unaccompanied minor, she arrived at A&E accompanied by just a teacher, as there were no interpreters and indeed no parents, but we sorted it. It took two years before she was able to convey that the last time she was nudged, it was by the butt of a gun before her mother was raped, her father taken prisoner, and her brother shot and killed. Experiences such as these always had to be taken into account.

Hampstead School prided itself on its equal opportunities policies, and always attempted to meet the needs of the international intake. However, it was not prepared for the different needs of children such as those who had been uprooted from their homes, or had experienced emotional and physical trauma and loss in war-torn and famine-blighted parts of the globe. These young people changed the way in which Hampstead worked. Our interview and induction procedures changed. The school started a buddy system to support all bilingual students and developed an after-school club where students supported students. Homework clubs and peer support systems became embedded in the curriculum.

The senior team had, as I did, a real passion and belief in equality and inclusion, and this allowed me to pressurize the local authority and fight for the rights of these young unaccompanied students at national and international level. I had to learn a massive amount in a very short time, knowing that while I would be supported in developing these initiatives, I would also be challenged to ensure that nothing I did would jeopardize Hampstead School and its students. A charity was born called Children of the Storm, to meet the needs of young refugee children. It was initially set up for those identified at Hampstead School, but it was expanded shortly afterwards to all such children, and we helped and supported other schools. Lectures and presentations, television and radio programmes became part of our extended working days. Hampstead became a leader in this field and secured National Lottery funding for the work. We wrote two school publications and produced a campaign leaflet and video, and they were made available for free to UK schools so that others could learn from our experiences. Fundraising for the staples that we all took for granted became an important whole-school activity. Sixth form students were on the management committee, and they took part in interviews and presentations, and trained and supported peers. 'It's the best work experience I have ever done', one told me.

What I loved about Hampstead was the ethos and passion for learning that inspired and enabled me. I learnt that setting myself the highest standards, expectations, and ambitious goals meant that those I cared for could be well taught and my teams would follow these beliefs and expectations. I learnt how to speak in public and how to challenge and be challenged. I learnt to be an effective team player, teacher, and communicator. I learnt how to take risks and the power of self-belief, self-esteem, and emotional literacy.

As for my past students, I still hear about their many successful achievements as authors, dentists, doctors, nurses, and lawyers, and their positive life experiences. Students I meet ask, 'Do you remember the time when…?' And yes, I do. I feel privileged to have been part of their lives. My refugee students are now scattered around the world, making their mark, rebuilding their homelands. It's good to know I have such wonderful friends around the world. Many have gained degrees and are working in their chosen fields as paramedics, nursery nurses, mathematicians, and one is now working for the UK ambassador in Bosnia. They all without question remember Hampstead School as the school that showed them kindness, support, and care in an intense and difficult time in their lives, taught them English, gave them a full and balanced curriculum, and also allowed them to follow their dreams, demonstrating most importantly the value of human kindness.

Leaving Hampstead was a massive wrench and the biggest risk, but I had been well taught and it was time. However difficult things became for me, I drew strength from knowing that given the right environment and ethos, we would be the best we could be. Today I run my own school, a testament to all I learnt. I hope that the ethos of my school resembles that of Hampstead School when I was there.

Jenny Depper

Teacher 1974–2008, including head of PE, head of house, head of year 1984

Currently mentor counsellor at Bushey Meads School, Hertfordshire
These are my impressions when I look back upon my time at Hampstead School. I have the fondest of memories and I am nostalgic for a school whose ethos and distinctive approach were special.

Any successful school has to provide a framework for its students and staff to thrive. Hampstead's special climate and ambience allowed this to happen. Gaining academic qualifications through a broad and balanced curriculum was not the only aim of the school. Our students also learnt socialization and how to be good citizens. Being steeped in cultural literacy and being allowed to communicate and express themselves freely were all within the curriculum and prevailed during the many and varied extra-curricular activities led by each and every department. The experiences provided were many and diverse. I have abiding memories of extraordinary drama and dance productions, with so many of the students and staff involved. As a result, interaction and mutual admiration between students and staff developed into shared respect within the classroom.

The school roll was truly comprehensive, as its children had different abilities, backgrounds, and cultures. They spoke over 50 different languages and brought with them a wealth of experiences. They were taught in mixed-ability classes in Key Stage 3 and for most subjects at GCSE. Teaching to the top and using differentiation enabled all the students to access the same curriculum and achieve to the best of their ability.

As a head of year I felt free to provide my cohort with opportunities to socialize through diversity. They attended theatre, dance, and opera productions. Dance students performed at Sadler's Wells and auditioned for free evening classes at The Place, with one of the boys eventually studying dance at Goldsmiths. Our students also contested Model United Nations competitions, engaging with, challenging, and winning against public schools such as Eton and Haberdashers'. Trips to Devon and the south of France, participating in water sports, climbing, abseiling, off-road biking, and other physical activities all challenged these city kids. And there were always parties – parties to say goodbye, picnic parties at the end of term, and finally, the farewell end of Key Stage 4 aboard a Thames boat.

I believe that the most important outcomes for the students were that each individual left the school empowered, fulfilled and independent. Some have gone on to be well-known journalists, actors, garden designers, cricketers, and footballers (ladies) representing England, but the vast majority whom we may never hear of, I am sure have become in the main well-educated, good citizens with purpose, direction, judgement, and the capacity to engage positively with everyone they meet. I worked with many outstanding teachers during my time at Hampstead School, but the people I remember most were the teenagers I taught. They were vibrant, funny, caring, intelligent, and a pleasure to be around, largely due to the fact that they had spent their secondary education as students at Hampstead School.

Mark Everett

Teacher 1994–9

Currently head, Writhlington School, Radstock, Somerset

> *After a heavy snowfall the more rigid branches of the pine break under the weight of the snow, but the more supple willow branches bend, thus allowing the snow to fall to the ground.*
>
> (Taoist proverb)

My story begins back in the 1990s – first a rejection, then an acceptance, and then a marriage – but that's just the personal side. I joined Hampstead School in 1994, after a year working in cheese factories and holiday camps. I'd been drawn to teaching following my decision not to enter the army and having spent a year trying to find my calling. In teaching I believed I had found it: at Hampstead I knew I had.

Hampstead was the second school I applied to. The first was an unmentionable place, where walking through the doors reminded me of a prison – no apparent love of learning, no smiles. I couldn't leave fast enough. Hampstead was different. From the first moment I walked through the gates there was a vibe, an excitement – young people with ambition and goals, and staff with passion and a sense of humour. It was a place where people worked harder than I had ever seen and played just as hard. It had its issues. It wasn't all rosy – it was fluid at times. Often the term 'organic' was used, but one thing was key: it was all about learning, and it was certainly a community of learners.

The strength in Hampstead wasn't the rules or the structures – it was in the people. There was a saying that certain people were 'Hampstead' people, and it was a range of people. There wasn't a mould for a Hampstead person. It was the quirkiness, the difference that made them. It was the belief in young people and the desire to give the job everything. At Hampstead I learnt my craft and learnt that teaching isn't a job, it's a vocation. I was looking for a calling, and I heard it there.

I was drawn to the school for its upfront approach – learning was at the heart of everything it did. It was less caught up with meaningless rules and structures that often prevent true learning conversations. Not everyone who joined Hampstead could cope with its nature. Those who did flourished, and others decided it wasn't for them. Rules came down to simple ideals: treat people as you would like to be treated; teachers expected to have ownership of their groups and classrooms; students were to be treated as adults, with respect. There was no uniform. Young people were free to express themselves, and express themselves they did. So many of the young people who experienced Hampstead during the time I worked there went on to be successful and do amazing things. Many became famous. The strength of the school was its comprehensive intake. Students came from a range of backgrounds, many disadvantaged, some very affluent, all of them Hampstead kids. Mixed-ability classes made you work as a teacher, but get more than the best out of the kids. Educational philosophy had driven decisions. However, seeing Vygotskian zones of proximal development in action (the difference between what you can do on your own and with help) with groups of young people converted philosophy into pedagogy.

I can remember my first-ever lesson with a Year 10 science class. It hadn't gone well, and on reflection I hadn't prepared properly. When I asked one of the students about the lesson at the end and heard the crushing – 'It wasn't quite good enough, sir' – I knew I had to step up my game.

The science teachers worked in the second-oldest part of the school, a complete block dedicated to science that became like a mini school within a school. We were a tight team, supporting and challenging each other. Key to the success was the collaborative way in which we worked, sharing good practice within our workroom, complete with its probationers' island where my still good friend George and I resided for a year, observed and supported by others in the team. The workroom became a hotbed of ideas and practical jokes.

Creativity was at the heart of what we did. We were lucky that we had a senior team and management that would support us in taking risks. We were accountable but encouraged to develop better practice. As I have continued to work in education and at many different types of schools, it has become clear to me that much of the work that was just expected daily practice at Hampstead has been rebranded as new ideas. Group work was just what we did. What became Guiding Practice was just a daily part of Hampstead lessons. The school was at the forefront of technology in education; all students data logging with class sets of laptops was something I was able to introduce in the mid-1990s into the department because I had the support. The school was using the web in education before most families had computers at home – 'broadband' was a term that nobody had heard of.

I was lucky enough to be given the opportunity to run a science week. Never having been able to do things in small measures, this whole-school event rivalled the many other designated weeks that the senior team was brave enough to entrust to young teachers. Sometimes things worked extremely well, and that tended to be when the staff pulled together. Sometimes things didn't work so well, but Tamsyn and the team would always look to the positive learning experience the kids had and build from that. There were times when the organic nature of the school drew frustration, but the frustrations mainly came from seeking constant improvement. My experience of other schools has shown me that being brave enough to take risks and place learning at the heart of what you do is the key to harnessing the energy of young people. Hampstead never stood still. For some that drew frustration, moving onto the next thing before the last was finished. But as I have experienced more, I can now see that the intervention on the sinusoidal curve of change was the key to the school constantly moving.

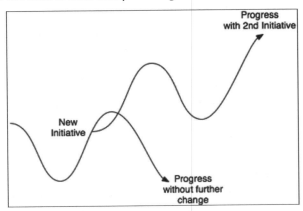

Figure 1: Sinusoidal curve of change

As a science department we were involved in the design of multimedia resources with international companies, acting as consultants to ensure the best learning experiences for the young people. We repeatedly entered and won national competitions, always taking a creative slant. We worked with researchers from prominent universities across London to improve our practice and demonstrate outstanding practice. We learnt as a staff. Some of us were encouraged and supported to further academic study, but all of us expected to share. The motto *Learning Together, Achieving Together* wasn't just a motto – it was at the heart of the school. When Ofsted said: 'Enthusiastic and energetic teaching generates an enjoyment for learning', I believe we could all recognize our school.

I have always felt proud of the time I spent at Hampstead and the things I achieved. I came to it with structures and rules, high expectations of myself and others. I learnt that embracing creativity and finding the spark to switch children on to learning is sometimes about flexibility. The strength of the school was in the people, their flexibility with a common strength at their core. As a willow they could bend in the wind, but they never budged from the idea that learning was the central purpose of what they did. Having the trust and investment from the senior team, the opportunity to lead and take risks, and the support from colleagues enabled incredible learning opportunities for the young people.

Despite having arrived with high expectations, I left with them even higher. I left Hampstead after five years, with lifelong friends and a lifelong partner. I moved on to a series of schools where rules took precedence over learning, and at times I found it difficult to adapt to their ways. As a new head teacher, I strive to create the best of what Hampstead taught me. Teachers I employ are selected in partnership with students. They have to have a passion for learning and an ability to transfer this onto the young people they deal with. Above all they have to believe in young people and that no matter the accident of their birth, all young people, given the best teaching, support, and guidance, can achieve greatness. I think I will always describe myself as a Hampstead person. And the rejection? Well, my future wife initially binned my application, but one thing I took away from Hampstead is to never give up.

Ruth Heilbronn

Teacher 1991–2000

Currently teaching and research, primarily in philosophy of education, Institute of Education, University of London

Parent 1981–95, two daughters, Lilah and Edna

I knew Hampstead School as a parent whose children had thrived there. As a teacher, I had my own reasons for wanting to be there. When I qualified as a teacher, Camden and Westminster were one administrative division of the ILEA and collaborated cross-borough on a spread of initiatives. We had subject centres for English and media, music and modern languages, among others, where colleagues met, developed curricular initiatives, undertook professional development, and worked collegially. Some of the initiatives from those collaborations were implemented nationally. I had worked in these arrangements under head teachers committed to the principles of the comprehensive school: Michael Marland at North Westminster Community School, and Ann Gittins at Pimlico School.

When the ILEA was dissolved in 1990, Pimlico became part of Westminster local education authority (Mortimore, 2008). Widely known as 'the Tory flagship borough', under the leadership of Lady Shirley Porter, Westminster adopted a view of education that included a teacher appraisal system characterized by performance-related pay. The job I was applying for at Hampstead would put me into senior management and in charge of professional development, with the remit of in-service and teacher training and the induction of newly qualified teachers. Appraisal was a hot topic at the time, and when preparing for the interview I rehearsed not only what I would say, but what I would do if I thought that I might be asked to adopt a Westminster stance. The question was put, and I understood from nods that my answer was acceptable. I later learnt that Camden's model of appraisal was based on development and developmental goals, and not on performance targets.

Over the next eight years I saw how this attitude to teachers and teacher development impacted on student learning. The head was committed to teachers learning together and students seeing them do so. She confessed in a school assembly to nerves over her MA studies, and told the students that she understood how they must often feel in class. She has written of the school-based MA run in partnership with the Institute of Education, University of London (IOE), which was committed to a view of teacher education based on the idea of a learning community – people learning together, and sharing and developing their knowledge and expertise. The partnership with the IOE was significant here, considering how many teachers in the school were involved in some form of learning, and particularly the school-based MA. Louise Stoll, one of the higher education leaders on this MA, has written extensively about learning communities and school improvement, and Chris Watkins' work further illustrates the power of staff learning together. Setting learning at the core of teachers' work helped to develop competence and expertise, but more importantly impacted on students' achievements, as it provided a model of active engagement with learning something new. At one time in the late 1990s, when the school surveyed the staff to find out what courses they were following, over 90 per cent were engaged in some form of professional development. This was verified by consultants when the school achieved an Investors in People award.

Hampstead School environment

1. Looking across the Quad to the Old Blocks: 'My husband happened to be familiar with some of the buildings, having attended Haberdashers' Aske's there before Hampstead was founded on the site in 1961.' Liz Williams, parent.

2. The 'New Block': 'We rounded the corner and faced what can only be described as a pebble-dashed panelled prison.' Mark Southworth, teacher.

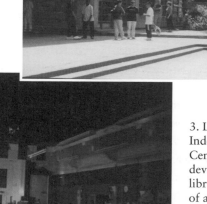

3. Library and Independent Learning Centre: 'The first major development came in the library with the creation of a new IT support area, the start of the development process.' Liz Williams, parent.

4. The Pond: 'This oasis, despite being tiny, was always popular and the staff had a great competition one year to find the most amazing ways of extracting water from it. I think Moira Young's team won with a modified vacuum cleaner!' Tamsyn Imison, head teacher.

Music – Hampstead style

5. A students' ensemble contributed to the first School Fair in 1985: 'Despite industrial action in 1985/6 we went ahead with ambitious whole-school events run by the children, parents, and myself.' Tamsyn Imison.

6. Alison Grant singing the Blues: 'On stage was, as it turned out, one future Amy Winehouse backing singer.' Andrea Berkeley, teacher and deputy head.

7. Joint concert with Trinity College of Music: 'Hampstead developed a total community of music makers during my time there.' Deirdre Broadbent, head of music.

Students and teachers

8. Tamsyn Imison with students in the library: 'Independent learning was how we described "homework", and I always enjoyed supporting children with this.' Tamsyn Imison.

9. Year 11 boat trip: 'And there were always parties – parties to say goodbye, picnic parties at the end of term and finally, the farewell end of Key Stage 4 aboard a Thames boat.' Jenny Depper, teacher.

10. School chat: 'Looking back, by far the best thing about it is its degree of loyalty among students and deep-seated friendships across year groups that still remain today.' Megan Smith, student.

Sports day – Hampstead style

11. Competition:
'We also enjoyed
competition
and challenge.'
Tamsyn Imison.

12. Heather and Jenny
on sports commentary
duty: 'I felt I was given
permission to be myself
and not fit a mould
established by the school.'
Heather Daulphin, teacher.

13. Cooperation –
Soren's tutor group:
'I was given the
opportunity to grow
as a young teacher as
well as being spiritually
engaged.' Soren
Jensen, teacher.

Learning Together, Achieving Together: Students' and teachers' learning

14. Phil Taylor teaching and learning from teachers: 'This was a genuine two-way process. Subject teachers brought a richness of curriculum ideas to the use of technology, while ICT specialists found practical ways to use ICT as a pedagogical tool.'
Phil Taylor, teacher.

15. Students' self-directed learning: 'Our approach to developing ICT hand in hand with subject-based learning and extended writing was also ahead of its time.'
Lindsey Rayner, teacher.

16. Sixth-formers' informal study: 'It was truly amazing to observe the transformation in confidence in formerly shy individual students at the end of this period.' Andrea Smith, teacher.

Creative arts at Hampstead

17. What you can construct with sticks! Arts Festival 1995: 'I will never forget the huge arts festival Charlie Cook organized for the whole school off timetable, and he was only in his second year of teaching!' George Reynoldson, teacher.

18. Professional artists in school: 'The third aspect that appealed was the creativity, which ran through the school like the words in a stick of rock.' Mark Mayne, teacher.

19. The dragon in the girls' loo: 'One thing Mrs Imison did early on was to get some of the older girl smokers, who had damaged the toilets, to paint the most amazing mural of a dragon on the walls and doors.' Ray Pathan, site and services manager.

To illustrate staff learning I pick three examples – work on developing assessment, initial teacher education, and the induction of newly qualified teachers.

Developing assessment

In the early l990s schools were coming to grips with assessment practices, building on the research and recommendations of the Task Group on Assessment and Testing. Phrases from that 1988 report that are now familiar and embedded in school practices were relatively fresh formulations at that time:

> Promoting children's learning is a principal aim of schools. Assessment lies at the heart of this process. It can provide a framework in which educational objectives may be set, and pupils' progress charted and expressed. It can yield a basis for planning the next educational steps in response to children's needs. By facilitating dialogue between teachers, it can enhance professional skills and help the school as a whole to strengthen learning across the curriculum and throughout its age range. The assessment process itself should not determine what is to be taught.
>
> (DES and Welsh Office, 1988: 7)

The head's approach was not to take an implantation initiative from the shelf or wait for directions from working parties to emerge, but to instigate a senior team away day, a back-to-the-drawing-board exercise in which we had to question the fundaments of educational assessment. This forced us to consider it in our context and to use our experience and judgement about what we ought to do in the school, in the light of this report. A similar exercise on an inset day led staff to develop a commitment to formative assessment in the early days of the Assessment for Learning movement, which all staff understood. An article on the process was subsequently published to disseminate to other practitioners. There was no blueprint at the time. A radical element of this conception was a marking policy that told teachers to mark less but mark deeply. Students were entitled to a deep marking at least every half term, with formative comments and a work review in which parents, governors, tutors, and the student discussed the work done and the targets set. This practice is now widespread.

Initial teacher education – valuing and supporting new teachers

Before school-based teacher training became obligatory, Camden LEA and the IOE developed an initiative, one of about four in England, based on a view of teacher knowledge and understanding that involved an entwining of the theoretical and the practice elements of the course. This included mentoring, formation of mentors, and a dialogical process of development. The process involved collaboration between a school leader (myself in this case), a visiting tutor from the IOE, and the student teachers working in school. We published a book about this initiative from which I cite Crispin Jones, then visiting tutor from the IOE: 'One of the important things about learning how to teach in inner city schools like Hampstead is that ... the excitement of teaching and learning permeates the school.' (Heilbronn and Jones, 1997: 83).

Newly qualified teachers

Hampstead's commitment to staff development is exemplified too in the support for newly qualified teachers, again in partnership with Camden LEA. Camden supported this work through its training and development centre. Work was done collaboratively across the borough, developing mentors (of whom I was one), developing an understanding of the principles and practices of good mentoring, and promoting peer development for the teachers themselves. Being a comprehensive school under the local education authority helped to sustain consistency in judgements and thus build the community of expert practitioners, which is a powerful driver of sustaining good teaching. I was a witness to the resources that were directed to this process, part of which was helping mentors to live our dual role of assessment and support – a difficult balancing act at times. Camden was acknowledged as a good practice borough in published national research at that time, and Hampstead was an exemplar in that study (Early and Kinder, 1994). What I learnt about staff development in general and newly qualified teachers in particular was later invaluable to me. I went on to do research on the effectiveness of the policy for the then Department for Education and Science, with a team from the Institute of Education (DfES, 2001).

The strong culture of professional development in the school supported me when I started my PhD. What I learnt at Hampstead laid a foundation for me to go on to work in university and continue in education on the same principles that informed work in the school.

Noel Jenkins

Teacher 1997–2003, head of geography

Currently advanced skills teacher, Court Fields Community School, Somerset

An observed lesson formed part of my interview process, and I recall that students clapped at the end, a gesture of support and enthusiasm that carried me through the rest of the day. I was delighted to be appointed in a school where students were so demonstrably supportive of teachers. The first year was a struggle, as it often is in a new school. Responsibility for a whole department weighed a little heavily, and I relied on generous support and advice from senior teachers and colleagues. The arrival of a uniquely charismatic and talented geographer in Tim Bown as second in department was the catalyst to a remarkable few years that I look back on with great affection and pride.

The geography department comprised a pair of classrooms separated by an office, an arrangement that enabled informal lesson observations and dialogues to take place constantly. As a new team, our immediate challenge was to raise the profile of the subject with the students. We weren't short of ideas, especially for active learning, from building a full-scale *favela* (Brazilian squatter settlement) in the school grounds as part of a creative day, to faithfully recreating the rainforest environment in a stock cupboard. The rooms were adorned with basketball hoops, props from school plays, a model river, and a constantly changing riot of display work. One room was enormous and lent itself to team teaching, which we practised whenever possible, especially with GCSE classes. We deliberately cultivated a degree of eccentricity in our efforts to create a subject identity. Students were welcomed to the classes with a variety of songs based loosely on theme tunes of popular TV comedy programmes such as *Shooting Stars*. Tim created an array of competitive games, the most popular of which was a golf game featuring an inverted overhead projector that was deployed to create a virtual golf course. The game became so popular that we organized an annual staff tournament for the Moira Young trophy.

Field trips were another opportunity to do things differently. We hired mountain bikes to study the limestone scenery of the Peak District. A level students found themselves modelling glacial landscapes from sand on wild Welsh beaches and reciting their own poetry on the streets of Toxteth, Liverpool. A GCSE enquiry into disabled access along the South Bank resulted in the temporary halting of the London Eye as students tested accessibility issues with a fleet of wheelchairs and threats of arrest from the Thames River Police once they reached McDonalds. I would highlight the use of new technologies as an area in which we were truly innovative.

When I arrived at Hampstead, my computer skills were fairly mediocre, though with the patient help and advice of the technician John Carruthers, proficiency improved rapidly. The policy of delivering ICT through curriculum areas freed up the time of the school ICT specialists to help us develop web-based interactive teaching activities that seemed to impress Ofsted in the 2000 report. We created a department website and focused on publishing student work, ranging from Year 7 poems to Flash animations, fieldwork reports, and synopses of A level research projects. Students were encouraged to write for a real audience long before the advent of the 'read-write' web and academic blogging culture, and *The Guardian* presented us with an award for our efforts in 2001. The newly emerging online communities enabled us to share ideas and resources with professional associations and colleagues beyond the Camden boundaries, and more than a decade later, I remain convinced of the value of professional development networking.

I should emphasize the role of student participation, which underpinned my whole time at the school. Time and again Hampstead students demonstrated a combination of eloquence, passion, and at times a quite subversive sense of humour. A group of students started a website to highlight the human issues behind global trade, and others held a conference with police and councillors to discuss their findings from a local street-crime mapping project. The Channel 4 comedian Mark Thomas filmed an episode of his show that saw Year 9 students debating working conditions in Indonesian factories with a director of Adidas, an MEP, and Indonesian union activists.

It was a privilege to take over the MUN debating club, which had been initiated by sociology teacher Donal O'Hagan. The school's extraordinary success in these events began at the Bath International Schools MUN in 2003, where Hampstead became the first state school to win, setting a precedent that has been repeated many times in subsequent years. It was fascinating to witness students becoming independent, politically aware citizens. Under the secrecy afforded by the stage curtain in the hall, they masterminded protest movements such as Hands Up for Peace and Messengers (an environmental poster campaign). Young people around the country were mobilized, together with a supportive mass media, friendly MPs, and lawyers, but crucially without any staff intervention whatsoever.

I was an experienced teacher when I joined Hampstead, yet in many ways it was the most formative time of my career. We were justifiably proud of our exam results, though just as important was our unspoken creed that real geography has real outcomes. After leaving, I moved to the West Country to teach in a small school in Somerset, with a county role in supporting ICT and geography. I maintain links with former Hampstead students and continue to publish teaching ideas and resources. I'm passionate about giving students genuine responsibility along with their voice, and MUN is thriving in our school. A lasting memory of Hampstead School hangs in my classroom: a photograph of UN Secretary-General Kofi Annan during the 2002 Earth Summit in Johannesburg. He is sitting below a Messengers poster.

I still pinch myself now.

Soren Jensen

Teacher 1990–2001
Currently senior teacher, Northgate School, Barnet

It was the early 1990s: the cinema was at Swiss Cottage, north-west London. The room was dark as usual but felt unusually cold, probably in line with the director's intentions of the newly released film, *Titanic*. I was a fairly young Hampstead School teacher from mainland Europe. I had young people on either side of me in the cinema from a huge variety of cultural and ethnic backgrounds. They were as silent as the stillness of the communal and darkened cinema room. There were moments where I held my breath and wondered how I would keep the troops together emotionally as I knew the storyline only too well. The young people had insisted that they needed to see *Titanic*. On my left were my form group; on my right, children from the Horn of Africa; from the former Yugoslavia, Mostar, Kosovo, Sarajevo; from Ethiopia, from Eritrea. The list of countries was long – too long – and reflected what was going on in the world. There were numerous moments during the film where individuals were intensely touched and their reactions visible. Others were silently sobbing, clearly moved by the work of Hollywood, and there were times when it was all too much, too symbolic a reflection of what was happening in their lives. They were children, in my care. Many were under 18, unaccompanied refugees. Just that night, and for a few hours, they were not just watching; they had been on board and I could feel their engagement and empathy with actors in the film.

I guess at the time, the world was very troubled. However, to my left and my right were children, just children, whose life circumstances had literally blown them away from their families, their homes, their friends, and homely circumstances. We therefore referred to them as Children of the Storm. They were being carried not by choice but by circumstance, and found themselves experiencing an unusual mix of emotions about the past, their current situation, and their right to hope for the future.

I recalled that earlier at Hampstead School we had watched the shelling and bombardment of Sarajevo, and still struggled to comprehend how we were only hours away from mainland Europe. I will never forget that night at Swiss Cottage, because all of us who walked out of the cinema had a peculiar seriousness in our conduct. The young people knew too well that when it comes to lifeboats, some make it and some may not, and I still recall the emotions of a level of guilt in the young people as we left the cinema: 'I made it – they didn't'. As former student Nerina from Mostar expressed it later: 'Those were the best and the worst times of my life', and 'You could smell it'.

My philosophy lecturer Mikkel at the University of Blaagard in Copenhagen once said of the story of the Good Samaritan that Western civilization has interpreted the meaning as 'doing good makes you a good person'. Whereas, he said:

> You could choose to believe that it's the person lying on the ground,
> the very person in need, who is the Good Samaritan, because (s)he
> gives you the opportunity to do good.

This affected me immensely, and it continues to guide my actions today. In regard to the Children of the Storm, I was supposed to be the teacher, but as with all the young people at Hampstead School, they also taught me a lot – we taught each other. They were the Good Samaritans giving us, the more fortunate, a chance to do what we thought was good.

Our slogan for Hampstead School at the time was *Learning Together, Achieving Together*. I still abide by that today. I will always respect the head teacher for weeding the playground in the morning prior to everyone's arrival. I sometimes wonder whether or not she knows how much of an impact that had on the conduct of students and staff. People often do not do as they are told, but copy. Hence we mirrored her behaviour around the school, so if we saw litter lying around the corridors we would pick it up. Sometimes learning does not hit you until years later, but the Children of the Storm, as all the young people I taught at Hampstead School, taught me about myself, made me grow as a person and a teacher, and I can only hope that I taught the young people something good too.

Describing how I even got to Hampstead School in the first place is hard. I was a Dane who was about to embark on my third and final teaching practice, and I suggested to my university lecturer that I carry it out in the UK, as I was interested in refugee education in a diverse society. He guided me towards Hampstead School and Athy Demetriades.

I am now an educational practitioner in the United Kingdom, still drawing on those valuable experiences from Hampstead School, where I was given the opportunity to grow as a young teacher as well as being spiritually engaged at a human level. I found it inspirational. It was a time when I would enjoy walking the school corridors during lessons because there was magic in the air, we knew it, and we all felt so very privileged to be part of it.

There were the excellent after-school clubs including Cocoa Club, where peer support was in full action, although we rarely used the term, and there were fantastic residential trips. Then there were the people: Penny and other cleaners who functioned as unintentional counsellors for staff at the end of the day. There were the heads of year, including Jenny Depper from whose pastoral outlook I gained vast experience; Ray, Aiden, and Paul, the site staff who kept the house in order; Pat Mikhail, the special educational needs coordinator (SENCO), and other heads of departments, whose knowledge filtered to so many people in such an inclusive way; the support staff Linda and Chris, and others who ensured that we all stayed mentally happy; the supportive PTA, with parents who took a real interest in their child's education. As a support teacher I was able to observe many remarkable teachers, and across the school I saw much innovative and supportive teaching.

The Children of the Storm that I met, taught, and still know were carried to Hampstead School by force. Most have since returned to their home countries. The storm carried me to the UK too, not by force but by choice, and that was a real privilege that I continue to appreciate. This may be the reason I am still here and they are not. My current upstairs neighbours are from Syria, and I am only too aware that the storm may be continuing for others. In any case, I continue to draw upon the significant human lessons from the Children of the Storm and the whole community of Hampstead School.

Margaret Johnson

Administrative staff 1993–present, head of administration, head teacher's PA

Currently school business manager and clerk to the governors

Parent 1993–2004

My son Gideon went on to complete a history degree at King's College London. He is currently working as a teaching assistant prior to pursuing a career as a primary school teacher. My son Nathaniel is currently working for Transport for London while pursuing further studies in music production and technology at evening classes at the School for Sound Recording.

In 1991 after a career break I decided to work within an educational setting. My own experience of education was not positive, so I was somewhat surprised by my choice. Retraining to become a teacher was not an option, and I researched how I could use my skills within an educational setting. As an experienced personal assistant working in the private sector, this was not a career path yet available in education. I therefore joined Hampstead School at a junior level as an administration assistant. My first impressions were that the lack of mutual recognition between professional disciplines was striking, and not one that I had previously experienced. This presented me with my first challenge: to change the perception of how administration staff were viewed, and the importance of their role in the school.

Working in a team of four, it quickly became clear what was at the heart of my initial negative perception. The 'general office', as it was then called, was rigidly controlled, which stifled the potential of staff working there. I recall being reprimanded on many occasions for leaving the office and talking to members of the teaching staff, and my social interaction with teaching staff was frowned upon. Despite these barriers, I knew that in order to understand the educational system I needed to understand the teaching profession and the internal and external influences.

Encouraged by the head Tamsyn Imison, who believed in lifelong learning, I was able to take advantage of career opportunities as they arose. Soon I was asked to stand in as the head's PA during a secondment, and I was later made permanent. When the administration supervisor retired I applied and was appointed to this role in addition to that of the head's PA. As administration supervisor and with the support of the head, I set about changing both teaching and support staff's perception of each other's professions. All reference to the general office was discouraged, and the office was renamed the 'administration office'. This had an immediate impact on the majority, although a small number remained cynical.

Local Management of Schools had not long been introduced, and it was obvious that the school was continually undergoing change that impacted on the delivery of the school's administrative services. The governing body was serviced by the local authority, and because much of the preparation for meetings was done at school level, the head suggested that I consider clerking one of the two meetings each term. I agreed to a trial period. This was an ideal opportunity to further explore and understand the education profession. In time I was appointed as joint clerk to the governing body and full clerk shortly after.

When my first child joined the school, I had to balance the challenges of being a parent and a member of staff, but with challenge comes opportunity. In this case it was to gain an understanding of education from a parental viewpoint, which helped me to understand the reason for change.

Hampstead School lived up to its motto *Learning Together, Achieving Together* then, and continues to this present day. At every juncture young people are encouraged to explore and grab the opportunities that are put before them, as well as ensuring that the academic requirement to continue their lifelong learning is not neglected.

Mark Mayne

Teacher 1997–2012, head of drama 1997–2000, assistant head teacher 2000–2; deputy head 2002–12

Currently head of Sir William Ramsay School, High Wycombe

The first thing that struck me about Hampstead was the compassion and the optimism that ran through the whole school community. This manifested itself in the trust and the strength of relationships across the school, and it was the first aspect of the school that appealed to me.

I had been privileged to have a wonderful insight into Hampstead prior to my appointment, through the school's leadership of the National Playwright Commissioning Group. This initiative was testament to the imaginative approach of both Jenny Johnson, my predecessor as head of drama, and Tamsyn Imison. Frustrated by the lack of new and engaging plays for young people, they coordinated 20 other schools across the country, including mine in Derby, in commissioning plays for each to perform. It was also an indication of the high expectation that lay at the heart of the school's community and its mission to provide the best possible opportunities for all students, whatever it takes. This aspiration was embedded then and remains a strong feature of the school to this day.

Hampstead's approach to democratic leadership was also exemplified in this venture, with workshops and shared performances in which students were expected to be at the heart of the creative process. In other words, students had a shared responsibility to drive the project forward. While many of us in other schools were beginning to explore the possibilities of engaging with student voice, it was evident that Hampstead students had come to expect to be a central part of curriculum opportunities and significant changes at the centre of the school.

The culture of the school was deeply responsive to student voice. I remember observing a school council meeting in my first term at Hampstead, facilitated by a senior member of staff and chaired by a student, and really starting to understand different ways to engage with students. It was a great occasion. Here was a group of students from across the years, discussing issues through shared procedures while maintaining a sense of hierarchy and respect. This exemplified the potential that every adult and student has to model behaviours and attitudes. It was a core part of the school's approach, and this became central to the way that I considered my own professionalism, and have continued to teach and lead others over the years.

A specific feature of the relationships between members of the Hampstead School community was the sense of friendliness that pervaded the culture of the school. This was the second aspect of Hampstead that really appealed. Many staff seemed to have the gift of maintaining a professional approach and balancing this with really good friendships. In some ways, the layout of the school – departments were isolated from each other – meant that the year rooms became the centre of the social fabric of the school. Year rooms, which seem unique to Hampstead and remain to this day, have always been a popular feature of the school, anchoring students into a particular group that enables them to forge a strong affiliation with other students. Many staff also gathered in year rooms at lunchtime as an opportunity to catch up with students and each other. The friendliness between staff was natural, and it included fun and laughter. Looking back, I see this was an essential part of Hampstead's contribution to raising life chances for students.

The third aspect that appealed was the creativity, which ran through the school like the words in a stick of rock. True creativity has always been at the heart of the most successful learning and leadership, and once I'd experienced the Hampstead approach, I wanted to be a part of it. Having stayed within the school as it has continued to evolve over the last 15 years, the challenge has been to retain this creative approach, involving principles of experimentation and connection. In the early years, Hampstead gave me the permission to experiment and connect with other colleagues. Both are about developing optimism for all young people in the face of an increasingly complex and challenging world. I explore each in greater detail.

There is no doubt that the creative approaches of others in those early years have contributed to the confidence and conviction I have to this day. I remember colleagues embarking on truly ambitious whole-school projects, combining subjects such as art and new technology, or music and mathematics, and this generated high expectations, collegiality, and connectedness across subjects. The culture of learning across the staff, exemplified by the MA group's work in conjunction with the Institute of Education, had a significant impact on the approaches taken by many staff. There seemed to be endless possibilities, and staff were receptive and keen to develop outstanding practice. I remember delivering some whole-school training within the first year of being at Hampstead, which is an indication of the school's approach to growing my potential as a new member of staff. There were two particularly memorable things. First, as part of the session I explored different styles of questioning, and challenged colleagues to ban hands up in their lessons for a week. The following day I was inundated with feedback from various members of staff. This was characterized by openness and honesty. While many were keen to experiment and explore different approaches, no one was saying that it was easy. There was an ambition to improve.

Second, I spoke in the training session about the need to give specific feedback to students and the dangers of global praise. At the end of the session I remember several colleagues modelling exactly what I had spoken about and giving me extremely detailed feedback, including the parts that could have been changed to improve it. This signified something that was central to Hampstead's approach to high-quality conversations through focused, productive teamwork.

Clearly, Tamsyn and Phil Taylor's *Managing ICT in the Secondary School* (Imison and Taylor, 2001) was important in both its content and what it reflected about the culture of the school. Here was proof that the creative approaches and connections between colleagues were always rooted in practical application and related to the context of Hampstead classrooms and student learning. While creativity through cross-curricular links was encouraged, Tamsyn was always adamant that each subject should maintain its own distinct ethos and approach. This felt particularly important for the arts subjects at this time. It created healthy competition, and we worked hard to upstage each other! I thought that I was doing quite well as head of drama with several big productions, and also the showcasing of some strong examination work in the drama studio, until my colleague, Deirdre Broadbent, head of music, decided to stage an entire opera, with students and staff. It was incredible.

The fourth aspect of Hampstead School that I found exceptional was the truly comprehensive mix of students. The mission to value every single student was exemplified across classrooms and also a range of extra-curricular activities. Within the classroom, nothing could be taken for granted about the life experiences, values, or aspirations of the students, and this created vibrancy in students' responses and demanded openness in one's teaching. For example, in drama I remember taking students who had never been to the theatre on trips with those whose family members were professional writers or actors. We taught schemes of work that included issues that had directly impacted on refugee students in the school, and were an essential part of their chance to reflect on these experiences as well as inform other students. Involving other languages within our performances became an important way to enable students to consider themselves as members of an inner London school with a shared identity while valuing their own individuality.

There was a rigorous expectation of all students regardless of background or particular need. At the end of my first week in school, I remember a phone call from Tamsyn in which she asked how my week had gone. We spoke about the learning environment and the curriculum, and a few of the changes that I envisaged. The call ended with her warning me: 'Don't underestimate the students'. In a sense, this became the motto that I have taken with me through the last 15 years.

So finally, the optimism. When I joined in 1997, there was a clear sense that the work of the school was creating better futures and embedding the culture of learning across each generation of children and staff. Valuing others and capitalizing on what we can learn from others was central to this culture, and this has spread across generations of families coming through the school.

I stayed for 15 years, and I hope that I carried the optimism of these early years through my work at Hampstead. Recently I have taken on the headship of Sir William Ramsay School in High Wycombe. In this new venture, I will be drawing on this optimism and also the creativity and high expectations that have become a central part of my outlook, ignited in my early days at Hampstead School.

Pat Mikhail

Teacher 1978–2009, including deputy head of girls' PE; head of learning support and faculty head

Currently consultant to Hampstead School, implementing the Achievement for All national programme

My original training had two strands, art and PE, and both have allowed me to support and offer learning in important complementary skills. I have always loved teaching PE, and for example, taking part in our exciting whole-school sports days, as well as encouraging competitive sport. These ensured every student was an active participant, working to improve on their personal best while cheered on by their classmates. Every member of the school staff took part in some capacity, which raised the status of PE in the eyes of the whole learning community as a vitally important area of the curriculum, one that builds physical prowess, confidence, dexterity, team spirit, and the joy of taking part. It was also a valuable support for many children with special needs, and for those who found they excelled more in their physical intelligences.

I was away during the intense industrial action, but came back in 1986 as a supply teacher, and was quickly brought into the learning support department by Judith Ryan. Judith soon arranged for me to go on the ILEA learning support course, a year's intensive training that took place after school. I was also offered day release for areas such as dyslexia, strategies for managing behaviour, and the integration of support with students having English as a second language.

We were fortunate to have a fantastic special educational needs inspector, Neil Smith, who is still providing invaluable support today. I could not have managed without him. He is an inspirational, calm, and positive LEA inspector, who is very supportive to the school. He held regular special educational needs coordinator (SENCO) forums for practitioners from all the schools and Lucy Adams, then head of Hampstead's special needs, took me along with her. Neil also provided funding for staff training and for us to carry out in-house research, which I was always keen to do, as it meant we kept at the cutting edge of good practice. We trialled different learning environments and new ICT equipment, including more portable laptops and dictaphones. In return for finance for investigations of good and evolving practice, we were required to give evaluations that were shared with other schools. For the LEA I also produced school policy and development papers that we discussed together with our colleagues in the other schools. Our main aim in the learning support department was to support children wherever necessary, so they all gained full access to the whole school curriculum, and to make sure we broke down the barriers to learning.

We felt it was essential to focus on the transition from primary to secondary to ensure that all children had full access to the curriculum and did not mark time or find lack of basic literacy prevented their enjoyable access to their lessons. I made it a priority to liaise with all of the 40 feeder primary schools – quite a challenge, but we did establish effective links with everyone. The heads of year set holiday tasks for the children to bring in at the start of the autumn term, and we collected work from feeder schools to demonstrate each child's level to our secondary colleagues. Our increased knowledge included important background and medical information and the identification of gifted and talented children. When we worked out the tutor groups, we took into account kindred spirits, placing children with a tutor whose interests would excite them, in order to get 'sparking points' or a father figure, for example. We also took into account their English as a second language needs as well as their special needs. It took us over two days to create harmonious and stimulating, supportive groups. We monitored these and, if necessary, would occasionally move a child.

Our learning support department was situated in the middle of our main teaching block, with a permanently open door. Being so central to the school, it attracted every student at some time and all the staff, who loved the tea, coffee, and biscuits. This meant it was seen as a very desirable place to be, and we arranged the suite of rooms to have open access to all our huge range of learning materials. The head and others were always admiring the feel in our rooms, the quality of our displays, our resources, and the masses of computers and ICT equipment. It was never abused, and children found it easy to use. We were open from 7:00 a.m. to 5:00 or 6:00 p.m., although I once frightened one of our site staff on early morning duty when I arrived at 6:00 a.m. He charged up thinking it was a break-in! As all children were welcomed, I might have one child at the first stages of reading alongside another one writing a book to be published. This made the department truly inclusive.

For a time, associate staff were known as 'bag ladies', as they had no real allegiance to the school, and came in and out, not under any direct control from us, carrying their large bags. We pushed for funding for teaching assistants (TAs) to be delegated to us. Once successful, we could create our own job descriptions and, when they were appointed members of our team, we could train and use them as vital members of student support. This in turn enabled professional development for TAs. Progression routes included higher-level teaching assistants (HLTAs), mentors, heads of years, and teachers.

For children with special needs, it was important that we worked hard from the beginning of their time at Hampstead to establish personal links with them and their parents. We would invite parents into our room for coffee and biscuits, and we went to the primary schools for statemented students' annual reviews. Better links with primaries helped enormously, and we had regular phone contact – I needed three phones in our room! I asked my team and other colleagues to always send positive comments home, and initiated home contact books so we and parents would know how the day had gone. For example, if a child had refused breakfast, we knew to get the cereal bowl out. In supporting children, we knew a small action could go a long way. If a plaster for a small cut, a hanky for a runny nose, or a drink for a tearful individual would help, it was given.

We supported 'quality-first teaching' in classes long before this term came into use, by helping subject teachers set appropriate work, explaining progression routes, knowing and using all the background information given to every staff member about their students, plus offering inclusion training. Professional development was always very high on the agenda. Class teachers needed to understand that if over 20 per cent of the children in every class had recognized needs, lessons needed to be planned accordingly. We prioritized safety, helping children to access and enjoy learning, and facilitate building their self-esteem.

Our challenges? Meeting some parents' expectations versus constraints, as there were never quite enough staff to go round. Paperwork and admin were a continual challenge. In addition, Hampstead stands on the boundaries of three local authorities, which meant liaising with the different home boroughs of the students. It was difficult to keep up. New children were coming in all the time, and we needed to test them all, have regard for their needs, and initiate immediate provision. The number of statements began as a handful, but over years these went up significantly to more than 50. At that time, children who had been in specialist centres were moving into mainstream schooling, and it was our duty to provide appropriate provision. This required much more training, and for facilities to be more accessible.

Initially we made use of our educational psychologists only for consultation and intervention, but because we were forward thinking as a school, we were keen to get them involved in curriculum development. For example, Mary Chamberlain and Ursula Cornish often took part in whole-school training and provided a different perspective on our challenges.

Our success was building a school that had an outstanding reputation for inclusion. I was really proud that we were praised in our Ofsted reports, and had a reputation with the LEA that we kept more youngsters in mainstream who would otherwise have been moved on. They always said it was rare for us to lose a child.

Being ahead of the game with ICT was invaluable for students, particularly those with poor handwriting and spelling difficulties. We also supported the development of ICT across the curriculum. In the autumn term we held highly valued strategy meetings for the new Year 7 classes. All the teachers and tutors came to a working lunch, where we discussed both individuals and group dynamics and shared positive strategies. All staff were receptive, and this meant we were able to catch things early and prevent much distress and loss of self-esteem. We had a brilliant working relationship with the school nurse, which meant referrals were quickly followed up. We linked closely with the English as a second language team, and became involved at a later stage if it was felt that a student also had learning difficulties. It could be quite challenging to identify these needs, as educational information often didn't follow these students, and tests needed to be conducted in their home language as well.

Changes at Hampstead from the 1980s into the 1990s included changes in demographics. Unrest in other countries had a direct impact on our intake and casual admissions. Also, internally accredited courses that we had set up and run to give special needs and disability (SEND) students additional accreditation were replaced by national vocational courses.

I particularly liked that Hampstead was such a diverse community – a true comprehensive. There was a positive vibe about the place. We were all learning and open to new initiatives. The joke that we had been involved with more pilots than British Airways was well known. It was a friendly, supportive community, and most importantly there was time to be proactive. Students exhibited an intellectual curiosity and a collaborative approach, and it was natural for them to support each other. There were always exciting things going on, and some of our productions were on a par with the West End. Staff at Hampstead were not scared of special needs, but open to changing their practice, and special needs children were included in everything. Hampstead always looked after the 'whole child'.

Sally Millward

Teacher 1998–2005, head of art

Currently assistant head teacher, Suffolk

When appointed, I initially struggled to identify with the ethos of the school. On the surface the school appeared to be relaxed and informal, as shown by the lack of conventional uniform, bells, and rules. However, as I scraped away the layers, a fast-paced, dynamic, and progressive comprehensive school was revealed that reaped the benefits of a diverse, creative, and vibrant learning environment. A shared mutual respect for the diversity of cultural, social, and economic backgrounds was embedded in the heart of the establishment. Everyone was rated highly, including staff. A few weeks after being appointed I received an envelope with a key, map, and note telling me to have a long weekend in the head teacher's holiday cottage in Suffolk. I felt appreciated and valued.

The students had a powerful voice within the school and were able to take the lead in many initiatives. They were given autonomy, and enabled to express themselves. This spilt out of the classroom, along the corridors, and into the community. Music appeared to be one of the conductors for self-expression, as students lined the corridors rehearsing through their breaks and lunches, creating impromptu performances. It made the school vibrate.

Not having confrontations about uniform focused attention purely onto learning. Classes were kept small – 21 students maximum for practical subjects, which enabled effective teaching. Productive relationships were formed with students in order to promote their individual skills and qualities. Experimentation, being imaginative with varied media, and risk taking were encouraged. I was continually amazed at the creativity demonstrated by my students and colleagues alike. It triggered a tangible excitement that made teaching fun, and I recognized that our success was due to our teamwork.

The students could be very independent-minded. For example, viewing an exhibition in London, I was surprised when my A level class unexpectedly turned up. They had overheard me discussing my plans with a colleague and organized the trip themselves. The same class achieved 100 per cent grade A, demonstrating a collective commitment, which echoed the school ethos: *Learning Together, Achieving Together*.

I enjoyed the engagement with parents who were keen to support the arts and creativity that the school cultivated. I actively encouraged their involvement and would speak to them regularly on an informal basis. Parents and other family members would eagerly assist with the public exhibitions and finding resources. Governors allocated to the department were also actively involved.

Students' personal and individual needs were catered for and supported through a strong and committed pastoral system. In order to enable Somali students to stay behind after school to develop their coursework, we opened up an informal crèche so they could pick up their younger siblings and return. Refugee students were supported financially so they could buy equipment and go on school trips. A special educational needs student with Down's syndrome achieved a grade A in art at GCSE and also at AS level. The exam board was called in prior to the moderation process to ensure that procedures were equal and fair. Her large portfolio contained a wonderful array of brilliant, colourful paintings that had an inherent naivety.

At the end of my first year, we held an exhibition of A level artwork in the beautiful historic environment of Hampstead Museum. Although the exhibition was a little ropey due to hanging restrictions in a listed building, the private viewing was a wonderful collaborative showcase of music, poetry, and art. Exhibitions of student work became annual events, though we changed the venue to Kingsgate Gallery, a smaller and less formal exhibition space for local artists, situated in an old warehouse that had been transformed into a warren of workshops.

We also developed close relationships with other local arts organizations, particularly Camden Arts Centre. As well as enabling our students to partake in regular artists' workshops, our relationship resulted in students being nominated for and winning national awards. As a department we gained opportunities to get involved with external agencies. I was aware that the school governing body and leadership team were pivotal in creating some of these through their networking and high levels of support.

Our annual trips to various European destinations were artistically fuelling and inspirational. Colleagues from different curriculum areas would accompany the art department and contribute to the overall success. We created darkrooms in bathrooms so students could develop their own films and photographs; art installations in hotel grounds; creative writing and poetry workshops on the coach; live blogs and exhibitions on our return. The older students took the role of mentors, demonstrating their commitment to art and organizing inspiring social events for the group. On one occasion, they booked out a tapas bar and sought live music so the younger students could appreciate an authentic and traditional Spanish experience.

With Technology College status, the school was keen for the art department to develop ICT, and organized this through in-class support with a creative, technical practitioner. Eventually the support mechanism was withdrawn, but by then we recognized how adept we were at using ICT as a creative tool. Exciting cross-curricular projects were rolled out across the school and in partnership with local artists and feeder schools. This heightened the creativity in our teaching, as software tools and skills were transferred across the curriculum. The art department integrated animation into Year 7 schemes of work, animating driftwood boat sculptures along choppy seascapes. Colleagues in geography would be using the same software with a GCSE class to show water sources and rivers, and A level physics students were using it to demonstrate energy.

The day before an HMI visit on creativity, a student won the local film festival with an entry entitled *Dinner on the Tube*. Excitedly, the class entered my room that I had set up as a private viewing room in anticipation that it would be difficult to settle everyone down. The inspector noted that it was important to respond to creative success and facilitate the opportunities for students to take creative risks in a safe environment.

Towards the end of the year I represented the school at an event hosted by the National Advisory Committee on Creative and Cultural Education, chaired by Sir Ken Robinson at the Royal Society for Arts in London, on the report *All Our Futures: Creativity and culture in education* (NACCCE, 1999). The focus was creativity, with eminent designers, celebrities, educators including Tamsyn, and politicians. I felt privileged to be given the chance to have an insight on how ideas and policies are formed at the top.

Hampstead was a high-profile school. Visits by television crews were a regular occurrence, and we were often featured on the news and other programmes. For example, television presenter Darcus Howe used the school to explore the differences between private and state education. He felt an affinity with the school, as his own daughters had attended it a few years previously. While my focus was enabling all students in my department to achieve, I enjoyed promoting our pupils' work beyond the school, and embracing the opportunities that occurred.

Being head of the art department for seven years left me with a wonderful array of memories – the only way I can describe the experience was akin to working at Hogwarts, a magical school. I learnt from a wealth of highly skilled colleagues and was inspired by the creativity of staff and students alike. I am now assistant head teacher in charge of teaching and learning in an extremely challenging school in Suffolk, but I have some Hampstead magic in my pocket.

Ray Pathan

Support staff 1981–present, schoolkeeper 1981–9; site and services manager 1989–present

On 6 June 1981 I began at the age of 20 as an assistant under the caretaker at Hampstead School. You didn't use your brain, there was no leadership and no management, and it showed. The caretaker came at 7.00 a.m. to our hut, collected his mail, and then said, 'Look after the shop, I'm going to play bowls'. That was the last we saw of him. There were no job descriptions, no line management, and we didn't really know what to do. The school looked terrible and the toilets were gross and unhygienic. There were huge amounts of litter and graffiti. It was embarrassing.

After Tamsyn Imison arrived in 1984, she would clean off the graffiti every night and pick up litter. She even brought her own cleaning materials and had her own cleaning cupboard. I used to help her, and I listened to her ideas for the future. We both knew that the school would only be good if the environment was right. One thing Mrs Imison did early on was to get some of the older girl smokers, who had damaged the toilets, to paint the most amazing mural of a dragon on the walls and doors in the girls' toilets. After that these toilets were never damaged, and the head always included them in prospective parents' tours. Sadly, years later, a temporary assistant misunderstood which toilets to repaint when I was on leave, and the mural was obliterated. I have never seen the head so angry!

After a second fire the caretaker left the school. In September 1989 I was appointed acting schoolkeeper, and with a lot of support and encouragement from the head – as I was only 25 – I was appointed to be the substantive site and services manager. I was given responsibility for all monies we obtained from lettings in the early 1990s, so I was able to carry out many minor works that considerably improved the school. Our first spend was £4,500 for CCTV and a set of walkie-talkie radios, which dramatically improved internal communications. It meant I knew where my team was, and the staff could access help instantly.

My major challenge was managing poor staff and building a good team, which mirrored what the head was doing. I had one who was 'permanently sick' but who we found was playing football. I allocated specific responsibilities and one building to each member of my staff, and provided work schedules with regular health and safety checks, which I monitored continually. The toilets soon became spotless, and graffiti was eliminated by rapid-response monitoring. Another nightmare was our cleaning contractors, over whom we had no control. They were quite useless and made ludicrous cleaning schedules that didn't work. One wonderful cleaner, Penny Haynes, brought in her own materials for months until the head negotiated for us to run our own service for half the cost.

One personal challenge I had was experiencing serious back problems. Mrs Imison invited in Sheila Lee, an ergonomics expert, to survey all the staff and student workstations. She insisted I was given a better office desk and a decent chair, and Mrs Imison gave me a much better, larger office that I am still using today. This transformed how I worked and felt. It gave me status and encouraged me to be successful. That visit did cost the school initially, but it paid off in staff well-being. Mrs Imison also paid for any staff with severe back problems to visit an osteopath, but this meant they got better much faster, and were away from teaching for a far shorter period.

I felt really valued by the head and staff, who came to me with wish lists to improve their department environments and create better learning facilities. We managed to carry out nearly all their sensible ideas. This also improved the whole learning environment in the school.

I have been involved in all the major improvements that have taken place from the mid-1980s onwards. I was often an unofficial clerk of works, for example when we won the Technology College bids, created our new Independent Learning Centre from the old Haberdashers' hall and stage, and carried out considerable restructuring within the technology block. My monitoring prevented work slowing down, and some things were done better. I do feel I have been key in many of the transformations of the school environment.

What I like most about the school is that it is always aspiring to be better and to go forward. I kept seeing the results. The main changes in the school environment were in the cleaning, the wonderful new library, and the four new science labs. Mrs Imison put in a request two years running for a partition across the large laboratories on the second and third floors. We were allowed this 'minor work', but of course the old teak benches would not fit in the two new spaces, so we ended up with two state-of-the-art science laboratories. When Camden took over, I was asked to advise on planned maintenance for the borough, which I was delighted to do. I was so proud because they valued my advice. I also particularly enjoyed meeting parents and visitors because they always made positive comments

My learning has been vital as I was surprised to be offered the job so young, but the head pushed and supported me, and I went on all the courses to be up to speed on health and safety, child protection, and new technologies. I have always enjoyed the learning that was relevant, and I never stop having to learn.

Over the years I saw the children dramatically change their behaviour in the warm, safe, clean, environment my team and I had created. These are my three priorities, my three golden stars: safety, warmth, and cleanliness. I fear for the future if the use of outside contractors will once again mean we cannot manage our own environment to get our three gold stars for our school community.

Comprehensive schools are for all walks of life, for everyone. Ed Miliband came from a successful comprehensive next to ours, and said he wouldn't have been Labour leader if he had not gone to one. Like many of our families, his were refugees.

Richard Pietrasik

Teacher 1988–91, deputy head

Head, Deans Community High School, Livingston, Scotland, 1991–9; CEO, Scottish Council for Educational Technology, director BECTA, head of education, BBC Digital Curriculum, 1999–2007

Currently education consultant (specializing in strategic leadership and ICT)

My appointment as deputy head came as something of a surprise. Full of high hopes, I had made my application, but the weeks passed without an invitation for interview. I was disappointed as it was exactly the kind of progressive, inner-city comprehensive I wanted to work in. Just as I had given up hope of being shortlisted, I received a telephone call one afternoon inviting me to attend an interview that same evening. Apparently one of the candidates had dropped out, and I was next on their shortlist. My response was ambivalent. I was pleased to be offered an interview, but since I had not been a first-choice candidate, I did not feel I stood much chance of getting the job. Also at such late notice, I had not visited the school or prepared for the interview, which would put me at a disadvantage. However, I was persuaded to go to the school later that day and meet the head teacher.

As I felt I was probably just making up the numbers, I decided to pull no punches when I spoke to the head teacher. I warned her outright that I was an NUT activist, editor of *Socialist Teacher Journal,* a passionate supporter of comprehensive education, and held very strong views on education, including mixed-ability teaching. My plan was to assess her reaction, and if she was not fazed by my views I would agree to attend the interview that evening.

Arriving at the school sometime after the school day had ended, I was struck by the amount of activity still going on. Groups of students were playing games outside, and in a number of classrooms I could see either a teacher engaged in some activity with students, or groups of teachers working together. People I passed smiled. The whole place felt calm and relaxed: a good place to work. My meeting with Tamsyn Imison reinforced this impression with a wide-ranging discussion in which, unexpectedly, she raised no objections to what I had to say. While not in total agreement with all my views, she pressed me to go for the interview, saying I would not be disadvantaged by being the reserve candidate.

I still felt I was the wild card, but having enjoyed my discussion with the head, I decided to be equally forthright in responding to questions from the interview panel. It was a liberating experience to respond so frankly and openly to their questions and not having to nuance my answers to avoid offending anyone or try to win them over, as would normally be the case. The interview went well, and the panel's response seemed very positive. The interviews finally finished at around 11 p.m. Just after midnight Tamsyn phoned: 'Wonderful news, Richard, we're offering you the job! You gave such a good interview that I'm going to buy a bottle of champagne for the candidate who dropped out!' And so began my deputy headship at Hampstead and three happy years working alongside Tamsyn.

Tamsyn Imison was a dedicated head teacher and an advocate of comprehensive education with a strong leadership style. This meant that every child in the school was valued and helped to reach their full potential. Hampstead was also very much part of the community and had a formidable and lively governing body, due to the nature of the community it served and the encouragement and responsibility that the ILEA gave its governing bodies.

The education management structure espoused by the ILEA had clear and strong supportive roles for national government, local authority, and governing body with the school management. This was a strength of our English education system. Now, the plethora of initiatives is continually undermining local democracy and local democratic control. It has encouraged overt and covert selection, left us with a developing hierarchy of schools, and concentrated power in the hands of the state. It has intentionally reduced the role of local authorities and the many valuable education services they provided.

Working at Hampstead was a great opportunity. The name leads many to believe that the school must serve a socially advantaged catchment, but while it serves part of relatively affluent West Hampstead, most of the pupils come from the very diverse and much poorer areas around the Edgware Road. While I worked at the school, 43 different home languages were spoken and a high proportion of refugees attended the school. The school ethos was that every pupil had great potential, and we encouraged them all to have high expectations of themselves. Young people from backgrounds that had no history of educational achievement were at all times mixing with children whose parents' relative affluence led them to have very high aspirations. In the right environment, this mix automatically raises many children's own expectations. Sitting next to another pupil who you can see is no better than you in class yet expects to go to university will automatically change your perspective on your possibilities. It is infectious.

I don't subscribe to the myth that great head teachers turn schools around single-handedly. It is much more subtle than that. Without good leadership, a school is unlikely to have a good environment for learning, but a school has many facets, all of which contribute to its success. It does a great disservice particularly to the staff of a good school to attribute its success solely to the head. Having said that, working as a teacher with a good head, who has a clear, enabling vision for the whole school community, makes the job very rewarding. In my case, as someone going on to be a head teacher myself, I learnt so much.

Tamsyn had a real clarity of vision and was always around the school encouraging and cajoling both staff and students to do that little bit more. She recognized how important the environment of the school is in creating the right atmosphere of learning and achievement, not just getting students to pick up litter but continually looking at how to improve the look of the school with a little bit of paint here or a picture there. Often she'd be the one with the paintbrush. After a minor fire in the staffroom, she took charge of its refurbishment to ensure it became one of the most pleasant spaces. It was a pleasure to sit there with its habitual buzz of animated discussion. Tamsyn recognized how important it is to develop that community of learning among the staff.

The staff were the real strength of Hampstead School. Talented and hardworking, they were a pleasure to work and share ideas with. They didn't just work hard in their own classroom or department, they all seemed to feel real ownership for the school and would involve themselves and argue passionately about any new initiative. Most people who choose to be teachers do so because they believe it is a worthwhile career – they have ideals. If, as a teacher, you find yourself in an enabling school community, a school that supports you and encourages your participation, there's no better job.

Schools have always been judged on their exam results, increasingly so in the last 20 years, to the extent that it has become an obsession detrimental to the whole school system. Hampstead's exam results have always been good, but a number of our neighbouring schools in that area of North London had better. There is nothing more galling than to hear people make a crude judgement about the quality of the staff at a school based on its exam results. The ILEA dealt with this by testing every child in their last year at primary school using the London Reading Test. Allocation to a secondary school was based on parental choice, moderated by an attempt to get a balanced intake and a good range of ability at each secondary school using the results of this test. The ILEA wasn't entirely successful in this endeavour. However, the results of the test were kept as a basis for assessing each school's 'added value' when the students' exam results from their GCSEs were looked at five years later. On the basis of this assessment Hampstead was one of the most successful schools in London.

One of my abiding memories is of sitting in my office early in the morning, well before school started, and listening to one of the students practising Mozart's Clarinet Concerto. As deputy head I was doing one of the most thankless tasks, the cover, but doing it listening to that music was a delight. My time at Hampstead was a great preparation for my next job as a head teacher of a comprehensive school myself.

Lindsey Rayner

Teacher 1991–9, history department, sociology

Currently deputy head teacher, Thomas Tallis School, Greenwich

My first substantive teaching post was at Hampstead, and it has been a touchstone in many ways for my subsequent teaching journey. Hampstead provided me with an insight into the ingredients of a good education. I benefited from being supported and coached by senior teachers, in particular Andrea Smith, Heather Daulphin and Anne Barton. Their coaching style and approach was an important element in supporting whole-school improvement and was helpful for me in developing my own preferred leadership style. The head too was very approachable and I always felt at ease in her office.

I think Hampstead students left with significant confidence and resilience, very like public school confidence, and something I had not experienced in my own education. There was strong social cohesion among students and they demonstrated great warmth. A critical mass of students appeared to have bounciness and showed fantastic creativity. For example, in drama, where the head teacher had organized for Adrian Mitchell and John McGrath to write plays for us and 12 partner schools across the country [20 schools were involved initially, with 12 taking part again], the students delivered challenging plays with a maturity that surprised us all.

The school was always looking outwards and bringing in ideas and opportunities from outside. Encouraged by Andrea Smith and Christine Counsell from the Historical Association, I was able to publish a paper on the use of ICT to support critical thinking and learning in history. This was a really important opportunity for me, for my professional development, and for deepening my understanding of how students learn and the concept of a learning community.

With our in-house MA we developed action research long before this became commonplace in other schools. This course was seminal and built us into a real community of learners as well as positively impacting upon the learning within the school. There was a strong emphasis on long-term continuous professional development. Everyone was *Learning Together* and *Achieving Together,* and this was something encouraged by the head, who talked about 'lead learners'. Chris Watkins and Louise Stoll (Institute of Education) opened up for those of us studying for the Master's a real interrogation of the processes of learning. This experience of action research and learning together moved my own professional development on considerably. The process of experimenting, sharing, and disseminating our research was hugely beneficial to me. In subsequent situations I have tried to draw on this as a key driver of school improvement. It was definitely an era and a school where things were allowed to develop organically. Visions emerged rather than being developed through a response to national programmes. However, the increased uniformity across schools and London in particular as a result of programmes from the National College for School Leadership (NCSL) and the London Challenge have helped to distil some of the very good things that emerged out of these times in schools like Hampstead.

We were rigorous for the time, while exploring and creating cohesive teams that developed creativity and innovation. However, we did not do everything right, and like many other schools at the time we definitely missed a layer of students, predominantly boys and often working class, who made slow progress at Key Stage 3 (KS3), sometimes did not catch up at KS4, and left us by KS5. At that time we were only beginning to have the technology and data analysis that today is commonplace. Now we can focus data and make sharper analyses on learning processes that children struggle with. This is why, although our results were good for the time (the 1990s), they would not have been good enough for today, when schools including Hampstead are achieving far higher results. The pressure to raise standards was not so sharply focused as it is today, and this gave us more space and time for collaboration. We placed greater emphasis on creating schemes of work, which we developed together. There is a very different inspection and reporting regime today and, while many teachers are worried that raising standards conflicts with creativity, I see this as our challenge today in comprehensive schools like Hampstead. We need to capture the collaboration, creativity, and pioneering spirit of those times while keeping a forensic focus on raising standards for all students. Exams are not becoming easier, but outcomes are qualitatively better as outstanding schools today have a much sharper focus on pupil attainment and progress.

The curriculum landscape too has changed. Today schools have more curriculum pathways and flexibility to make early, effective interventions for students, another key factor in raising standards. Hampstead was fully comprehensive. Supporting all students to make a successful transition from KS4 to KS5 was something that we identified as important. Andrea Berkeley's *History of Ideas* course provided our sixth formers and staff with an amazing experience, giving a joined-up framework of understanding for all the A level courses. The students gained a fantastic educational experience.

I left Hampstead acutely aware of the gaps in students' knowledge and understanding that can hold them back. My involvement in this also helped to shine a light on the importance of a flexible curriculum, responsive to the needs of students. I do not think that the blanket approach to mixed-ability teaching is something I now adhere to, but nevertheless Hampstead is where I deepened my understanding of how to differentiate materials and resources to support all learners to achieve learning outcomes.

At Hampstead I remember the pioneering attempts to identify gaps in the students' learning: for example, when I left Hampstead, I found that the literacy work done by John Sullivan, Karen Melia, and Joanna de Regibus in the English as a second language department was ahead of its time. Our approach to developing ICT hand in hand with subject-based learning and extended writing was also ahead of its time. This can be attributed partly to the careful attempt by the school leadership to ensure that Technology College status contributed to the learning across all departments.

Another important feature of Hampstead was the emphasis on the student voice, with the strong student council and their involvement in the appointment of staff. The school council was trained to use Socratic dialogue to discuss ethical issues and put forward strategies for improving school procedures such as preventing bullying, with peer counselling for the bullied and the bullies. School leadership was demonstrated at every level from students, staff, and the senior team.

After leaving Hampstead I worked in a new school as head of humanities for three years, followed by four years in Brent as a foundation consultant and coordinating the secondary strategy team, where we were focusing on pedagogy – teaching and learning, and using data to drive up school improvement. I then worked at the Convent of Jesus and Mary Language College in Harlesden as assistant head teacher for teaching and learning, another real learning curve. Autumn 2012 sees me as deputy head teacher at Thomas Tallis School in Greenwich. Here I see my challenge as how to raise standards for all students while developing a creative curriculum that supports all students in making fast progress, in a way that develops the confidence, resilience, and bounciness that I first saw in students at Hampstead School.

Joanna de Regibus

Teacher 1991–present

Currently head of English as an additional language

I have always loved the atmosphere at Hampstead School. The staff are friendly, approachable, and passionate about teaching. When I started teaching at the school I received a lot of support from my line manager, Athy Demetriades, and senior management, who gave me the freedom and flexibility to work in the way I wanted to for the inclusion of ethnic minority students. We never worked in isolation but always in teams. We were valued for our hard work, and became an integral part of the school, always consulted as experts on language matters.

When I joined the school I was supported in gaining qualified teacher status, as my Polish qualifications were not recognized here. Being a foreigner and speaking several languages has helped me to understand the position of those children who came from abroad, and as I have an MA in applied linguistics, I can understand the principles of second language acquisition.

As a team I believe we have made a difference to the lives of ethnic minority students, particularly vulnerable refugee pupils. For us, every child really does matter. Over the years, I have been able, with my team, to establish a unique system of networking and guidance with mentoring. From the 1990s, English as a second language support has transformed from being an add-on to becoming an integral, powerful lever for transforming learning across the school. Language support and in-class support are delivered in partnership with mainstream teachers, and we often take the lead in whole-class delivery.

We still practise our credo, developed together in the 1990s: *Learning Together, Achieving Together*. There is much theoretical and practical learning going on for newly qualified and beginning teachers, and we are all continually learning to improve upon and develop our teaching practice to support our children with English as an additional language. Like curriculum support, we have a welcoming central room open at lunchtime and after school that is used by all because of its infectious learning ethos. We have always valued the culture of each country, and the wonderful whole-school celebration events that began in the 1990s are even more amazing today. Over 300 people from the school and the local community attended the last International Festival at Hampstead School, which featured in local newspaper articles.

Hampstead runs twilight sessions for teachers to share our latest ideas. I recently presented on grammar and differentiation to many staff who had never experienced discrete grammar lessons themselves. We no longer just support teachers but are also co-partners in delivery with subject staff. I work closely with heads of department to support students new to the country by teaching language skills and subject-specific vocabulary and concepts (induction programme for newly arrived EAL students). We now regularly share our good practice outside the school by presenting at conferences.

With recognition for exemplary practice in support of the national strategies, our department featured in a Department for Education DVD, *New Arrivals Excellence Programme Guidance* (DfES, 2007, part of the *Primary and Secondary National Strategies*), which was used to train teachers across the country. Currently I am working on a fast-track literacy programme for students below level 4 upon entry. With the maths department we were involved in work on the minority ethnic achievement project (MEAP), to make the language of exam questions intelligible and accessible to these students. These strategies also benefited monolingual students in maths lessons. As a result of the MEAP interventions, our Somali students had the best results in Camden and nationally (2007), and we shared our strategies at conferences.

The team has been very successful at raising the achievement of Somali students at Hampstead, thanks to the work of our Somali home-school link worker. We have developed strong links with the local Somali community and work closely with Somali parents as the best way of increasing their children's motivation and developing relevant learning experiences. The school and the team's work in the field have been cited in good practice research (e.g. Demie *et al.*, 2008; Rasmussen, 2011).

George Reynoldson

Teacher 1994–9

Currently teaching science, Camborne Science and International Academy, Cornwall

I was brought up in West Hampstead and went to Holy Trinity Primary School. At that time we either went to Quintin Kynaston (QK) or Hampstead. I went to QK because my father liked the head, Peter Mitchell, but he only stayed for three years. I had lots of friends at Hampstead and they all did well. I liked Hampstead School when I spent a week there beforehand on a placement. The staff were friendly and welcoming, and the department was well organized. I spent a lesson with each teacher and saw some excellent teaching. Jonathan Bach was our head of department.

I felt privileged coming to Hampstead as it was a place that was well rounded, confident, friendly, and warm. It welcomed a wide range of student achievement levels and aimed at engaging everyone in enjoying learning. Everyone was expected to stay on post-16. Hampstead expected to help students become independent learners, not to spoon-feed them. It was not too formal – staff and students looked smart but were not in uniform. There was a nice balance. You saw everything as it was, nothing was hidden. Problems such as bullying can be covered up with uniforms. The students always expressed their views very strongly on what was right and wrong. Through the school council they set the rules, so they did not break them.

I am always most proud to meet up with former students, who are always really friendly. I was lucky enough to see my tutor group right through the school, and then when they had left I saw that they were putting something back into their community, as I was trying to do. They are still all friends. We were very much a community school, and at Hampstead I learnt the importance of working in a team.

In my lessons I enjoyed the challenging questions I was asked that stopped me in my tracks, making me learn. *Learning Together, Achieving Together* is really important. It was rewarding seeing eureka moments occur for students. We had lots of things going on after school, such as the rocket club run by Simon Hunt, where we launched quite ambitious rockets in the University College school field behind our school. It was often almost too exciting. We also had some fire eating demonstrated by one member of staff! (He had been trained.) Our A level student investigations were exciting when the students came up with the questions they wanted to work on. One was to investigate the probability of building a ship over a certain size while retaining its efficiency. Another was exploring chaos systems where a girl suspended a pendulum between two magnets. She was awarded the Best Physics Coursework Prize for that year nationally from the Institute of Physics.

So many staff sent children through the school that it showed we all believed in the school. We wanted the best for all of our students and usually got it. We had many creative and talented teachers. Staff were very proud to be at Hampstead and felt they made a difference. It was quite magical. Staff really valued all the children. We were all really good friends. We felt empowered to do things and innovate. I will never forget the huge art festival Charlie Cook organized for the whole school off timetable, and he was only in his second year of teaching! It was really inspiring. We painted one of our old science labs as a jungle room. We also had strong drama links with both the Tricycle and Hampstead theatres.

After I left Hampstead I worked in Japan in the International School there. It was also cosmopolitan and had many similarities to Hampstead. I think we all have really fond memories of being at Hampstead.

Andrea Smith

Teacher 1989–2010, including roles in the history department, assistant head with responsibility for the sixth form, 2000

Currently training and supporting middle leaders working in schools in challenging urban contexts

I knew Hampstead School's reputation as a good neighbourhood school, and as I lived within half a mile it seemed like a good place to teach. I joined the school initially as a supply teacher in the history department, and then stayed for the next 20 years! During that time I progressed from part-time teacher in 1989, to second in department, head of department in 1995, and finally assistant head with responsibility for the sixth form in 2000.

The challenge I faced as head of history was a dual but interrelated one: how to ensure that every student achieved her or his personal best, and that every child enjoyed learning history. In my view, the first was not possible without the second. The most pressing challenge seemed to be the design of a curriculum that could appeal to the wide variety of students in a typical class. These included a high proportion from recently settled families, and included refugees from areas of recent upheaval or political suppression such as Somalia, Bosnia, and Iraq. These children were often from educated and aspirational backgrounds. Other students came from longer-settled populations, also widely differing in social background and aspiration. We were acutely aware that history was a significant and highly sensitive subject that sought to make sense of the turbulent road to the present, and a subject that permitted, and even celebrated, the different interpretations of that journey by encouraging logical discussion and debate. Furthermore, it was a subject at the heart of improving communication and other essential literacy skills at all levels.

The problem was how to engage the interest and motivation for all, for without both of these ingredients no learning would take place at any level. It was not enough to leave it to the clinical and rigid strictures of the national curriculum, though this certainly had to be followed. So we did more than was called for in the national curriculum. We taught medieval Britain, but designed homework assignments that invited studies of contemporaneous histories in other countries. We might study seventeenth-century Britain, but set structured homework assignments on other examples of inter-communal conflict. We studied industrial Britain, including the expansion of empire, but also explored the histories and experiences of colonial peoples. We were proud of teaching students how to learn history with all its rigorous critical processes, resting as it did on the balanced presentation of evidence and critical evaluation of sources.

What was frustrating was the arid debate being pursued in the press. Were we part of the errant group of teachers who betrayed the subject by teaching skills to the detriment of historical knowledge? This was a cheerless debate whose appeal lay in its reference to some form of populist traditionalism, and certainly not in the rigour of any university history department.

The success of our approach was evidenced in the number of students who chose history as an option at GCSE, the many students who chose to continue their study at A level, and the healthy number who chose to continue their historical studies at university.

The challenge as director of post-16 studies was different, as the underlying ethos of a sixth form in a comprehensive school is essentially different from that of a selective school. In a selective school, an assumption is made that the sixth form prepares students for entry to university through a programme of A levels or baccalaureate. Students have to prove themselves worthy of entry to the sixth form by achieving high grades at GCSE, probably

A*–B grades. In a comprehensive school, every leader would like to think that the purpose of the sixth form is to provide continuing opportunities for educational achievement for as many of its Year 11 students as possible, whatever their prior attainment. Therein lays the essential challenge. It is simply not viable to run courses for small numbers, so difficult decisions have to be made. How far can a liberal curriculum choice be maintained? After all, students will achieve well if they study what interests them. What are the maximum class sizes that can be sustained? What are the minimum? How thin can the butter be spread? This essential challenge was enhanced by the diversity of Hampstead's student body. We wanted to provide a sixth form that would offer each student an enriching experience, excellent qualifications, and a smooth pathway of progression to higher education or meaningful employment.

Most students were of course drawn from our local area of West Hampstead and Cricklewood, areas expanded both at the beginning and the end of the twentieth century by waves of inward migration. Many new students were attracted to the sixth form by this diversity, and we drew applications from many diplomatic families or families of the local academic community. So the profile of the students was diverse, including young people from areas of recent political upheaval, such as Eastern Europe and Somalia, as well as longer-settled families from countries of the Commonwealth and regions of the United Kingdom. We were fortunate. The vast majority of all our students were highly aspirational and valued educational opportunity.

For many students their path was a smooth and traditional one – it was merely a matter of selecting an appropriate programme of A levels that would lead them through to university. The school had a long tradition of providing a good range of subjects, taught by experienced teachers with results that opened doors to the best universities. For most of our students, this was still an appropriate pathway to choose. Many a talented student went on to an elite university, and many more to destinations carefully chosen for their excellence in subject teaching. However, times were changing, and for an increasing minority the path was not so obvious. Many had not achieved highly at GCSE for a variety of reasons. Some had experienced real trauma and sudden upheaval from their homeland. Others simply had not been in the country long enough to develop their literacy skills, and others came from socially disadvantaged families unable to support their children through the lower levels of school. Many of these students were not in a position to join an A level course. So for different reasons alternative provision had to be made. These young people had first to consolidate the level 2 skills they needed before they were in a position to leave school and join the workforce or to embark on further qualifications. We targeted these students during Year 11, and with our careers adviser actively put pressure on them to remain in our school. So we looked to expand our range of level 2 vocational courses, where learning these important basic skills could be reinforced and tested in a supportive environment, while at the same time nurturing more advanced analytical skills that would prepare them for the next stage. Language support was provided whenever funds would allow. It was intensely gratifying to see many students progress to a programme of A levels the following year and thence onwards to university. But it was also pleasing to see formerly reluctant and even truculent students mature and develop sufficient confidence and skills to apply to colleges of further education where they could pursue their ambitions further.

However, as the new century progressed and in response to student demand, it became evident that we would have to also review our level 3 provision. A levels provided well for many students, but an increasing number were expressing interest in, and aptitude for, the newer vocational level 3 courses that offered an alternative pathway to key areas of employment. We added health and social care, performing arts, engineering, and financial studies to our existing provision of business studies and information and communications technology. These courses were hugely popular and expanded as they proved their worth by delivering excellent results and winning students places at university. They were attractive to many, as the progression paths to employment were obvious. London University students provided mentoring support, and many ex-students returned to speak of their successes after leaving school.

The quality of teaching and learning was always of paramount importance, and it was essential to track and monitor the performance of each individual student and provide support and encouragement when necessary. A caring team of tutors directed by effective heads of year usually took care of individual student achievement, although adolescents could be remarkably headstrong at times, much to the consternation of their parents and tutors. Teachers were always encouraged to ensure that their academic knowledge was kept up to date and the school was generous in its financial provision for attendance at appropriate courses and lectures.

However, we also recognized that it was essential to broaden the horizons and experiences of our students. So tutors and teachers were encouraged to run extra-curricular activities. We were proud of our debating team that brought home trophies from national events, societies that organized events for raising awareness for local and national charities, and various clubs devoted to sport or games. Students had to complete a Community

Challenge that required 15 hours of voluntary service with a local charity or organization, or simply to support academic achievement in the lower school. It was truly amazing to observe the transformation in confidence in formerly shy individual students at the end of this period. The vast majority continued their commitment far beyond the minimum period. When I left, I was happy that sixth-form numbers were buoyant in an ever-competitive environment, provision was balanced and cost effective, and the sixth form was judged to be within the top 10 highest-achieving schools in England.

I am proud of all of this, but most of all I value the friendship and camaraderie that the students say is the enduring legacy of their time at Hampstead. I liked the palpable ease with which all the diverse groups of students within the school mixed together. In the sixth form common room, there was genuine interest, regard, and at times, open affection displayed. Break times were loud and exuberant, and rang with tales of shared experiences. Students were always highly supportive of each other. Friendships formed in school endured into adulthood.

Since leaving Hampstead School, I have worked with an organization (Teaching Leaders) that trains and supports talented middle leaders working in schools in challenging urban contexts. As a coach, I have the privilege of visiting schools and meeting students who are full of hope for their future and who depend so much on the vision, leadership, and commitment of teachers to support them in their educational journey.

Mark Southworth

Teacher 1996–2002, deputy head

Currently head teacher, Woodcote High School, Surrey

After Finchley Road station, the Jubilee line emerges from the tunnels of central London. It rapidly climbs to an elevated section over dense housing and semi-industrial landscapes partially shielded by the buddleias growing through cracks in the concrete that also partially obscure trackside graffiti. I looked again at my interview letter. I had expected to be on the Northern line – surely Hampstead School would be near Hampstead Tube station? I had been there several times and remembered the village feel and the sense that you could have been in any part of rural England. In many ways, I hoped it would be like Oxford, where I had spent the past 10 years.

My teaching career so far had been lucky. I got a job in the school where I did my PGCE placement and had been promoted three times. Sitting on the Tube, I realized that my experience of educational interviews was limited. My interview for the full-time job in my placement school was informal, tacked onto other interviews. I was called in to the head's office, greeted by the chair of governors and the deputy head, and after some small talk the chair announced that he hoped I'd be happy in my new job. At this point the head entered the room from his private facility to be told I'd been appointed.

The deputy head job at Hampstead School was different. It was advertised in the *TES* and there were formal interviews over two days. I'd got an early Tube and wanted to walk round the area. I checked my letter and noticed a woman opposite, dressed as if for an interview. 'You here for the job at Hampstead School?' she asked. (Was it that obvious?) 'I can see the interview letter.'

Just what I needed, bumping into another candidate on the Tube! But it was Anne Barton, one of the deputy heads, who offered to walk me to the school. Marginally better than a competitor, but bang went my chance to see the local area. We got off at Kilburn station, about 15 minutes' walk from Hampstead School, past a typical landscape of Victorian and Edwardian houses nestled against post-war social housing. 'The ideal catchment of a true comprehensive school', Anne said. 'I suppose they called it Hampstead School to make it sound appealing, but it's a long way from the village or the Heath.'

We approached a not unattractive Victorian red-brick building with steeply pitched roofs, arched windows, and a spire – the sort of building that would make desirable loft flats, full of light and original features, near the Tube and 25 minutes from the West End. With a gravel drive, surrounded by rugby pitches and a cricket field, it might have been a minor public school, the Hampstead School of my imagination. But there was no sweeping drive and no sports fields of any kind. The school was feet away from the road, overlooking 1970s council flats crammed between the road and the Thameslink line to Bedford. The school's façade suggested faded grandeur with its stone coat-of-arms. Like many schools of its type, there was no obvious entrance. I was grateful when Anne led me through a gap proclaiming the way to 'the central quad'. Central quads have been essential features in school design for as long as there have been schools, and for a millisecond I pictured myself entering a space transporting me back to the Oxford colleges. I made a mental note to keep off the lawn. I needn't have worried. There was no lawn.

We rounded the corner and faced what can only be described as a pebble-dashed panelled prison. In the 1960s the ILEA had clearly decided to enlarge the school in as utilitarian a way as possible. The only thing saving the architect's shame, and perhaps his job, was that his work was not visible from the road. Taken from the book of Brutalist architecture and with value engineering clearly applied, the building loomed in its Eastern Bloc glory.

A later decision to paint the Crittall windows in a red oxide gave them the appearance of rusting bars from which there was no escape.

We crossed the quad and entered the New Block, as I later found the distressing edifice was called. With over an hour to go before the interview, I would have liked to have gathered my thoughts or even run away, but I was ushered into the head teacher's empty office. The interregnum gave me a chance to think. 'This was not what I was expecting, but I'm here now; at least it is good experience for future interviews. My application for Pimlico School is in the post, and that is certainly in a posh area.' The room was surprisingly cosy and cottagey, and dominated by three large, pink sofas. Curtains and nets softened the Crittall windows. The corner aspect of the office allowed light to flood in from two angles and gave a glimpse of the first bit of green space I had seen at Hampstead. A display cabinet with a curious mixture of knick-knacks, students' artwork, and framed certificates overlooked a large and slightly untidy desk in the corner. I sank down on a sofa. The door opened and I tried to struggle to my feet, my plastic wallet with the instructions slipping between two cushions. What should I call the head? She looked friendly. We could get on. Anne had referred to her as Tamsyn, so Tamsyn it would be. I held out my hand and heard in reply, 'Hello, I'm Margaret, Tamsyn's PA, welcome to Hampstead. Cup of tea?'

The pink sofas were to play a large part in the interview process, and for that matter the next few years. From the relatively lofty position of her desk, Tamsyn addressed the candidates who were sinking into the cushions and told us we would later be joined by three internal candidates. Looking every inch a leader, she seemed to be sizing up us externals to see if anyone could possibly measure up to the people she had trained, mentored, and honed over the past few years. She was a formidable presence, draped with amber jewellery to match her amber hair. 'I won't tolerate underachievement at Hampstead', she said. 'We had excellent results last year with five students into Oxbridge, and all Year 11s going on to further education. This present exam group is not as bright, but this is not an excuse for failure. I simply won't tolerate it.'

With this, she put a mark in the sand that said: 'This is what we are about. I hope you're up for it. If you're not, leave now.' Several candidates took the hint and fell by the wayside over the next two days, but the more I saw of Tamsyn and her school, the more I wanted to be part of it. Touring the school is an essential part of the interview process, and I was shown round by a Year 8 student. 'Ask Magid to show you the whole school', Tamsyn said:

It's not a tour of corridors; get into classrooms and see the learning. Make sure you ask plenty of questions about what it's like to be a student here. This is your opportunity to see if it's where you want to be. It's a two-way process: we want the best candidate, but we want someone who is passionate about what we do here.

What struck me during the following hour was the diversity of the students in the school. In perfect English and in a softly spoken, hyper-polite way, Magid told me he was from Sudan and loved music. But not rap or hip-hop or any other type of street music; he liked classical. I learnt later that he was typical yet untypical of the students at Hampstead. In truth, there were no typical students. This became obvious as we wandered in and out of the purposeful classrooms. There was no overriding ethnicity, class, and home language. The lack of uniform and bells grated against my traditional background, but as we toured, I began to see that this system worked. Liberal certainly, but also focused and academic – a system geared to helping youngsters achieve, no matter what their starting point.

We arrived at the House, a small detached ex-caretaker's dwelling shoehorned into the far corner of the site, which mirrored the architectural wretchedness of the new block. It was little changed from its former incarnation, with a semi-fitted kitchen, brightly coloured bathroom suite, and small rooms with swirly Artex ceilings now hung with fluorescent strip lighting. The rooms seemed to have been entirely furnished by IKEA. In each, four or five students were engaged and busy working with an adult, with resources that seemed more at home in a primary school. The rooms resonated with accents from all over the world. I met Athy Demetriades, the refugee co-ordinator, and then Soren Jensen, who was working with some Somali refugees. Athy told me:

They are mainly from Mogadishu. Many have arrived in England unaccompanied, trafficked into the country, and were left at the border. There is an increasing issue from Pristina, with ethnic Albanians fleeing the ethnic cleansing in Kosovo. We've set up a charity called Children of the Storm, but we need more funding. We've applied for a lottery grant, and Griff Rhys Jones has agreed to hold a fundraiser for us next week. You must come – er, if you get the job!

Later, Tamsyn's voice on the telephone congratulating me on getting the job sounded genuinely delighted. 'You've got five years.' (Mixed emotions: I've got a deputy headship, but is it a fixed-term contract? I don't remember seeing that in the small print.) 'Then you must apply for a headship,' she continued. 'I want my senior leaders to be ambitious. My last two deputies are now successful heads.' This was Tamsyn drawing another of her lines in the sand. 'I know you don't start until September, but there is so much to do. You must come to the fundraiser tomorrow; the charity is so important to us, and is really making a difference to our refugee students. Now, we need to discuss your job description.' Having only just internalized the job offer, I would have liked more time to reflect, but I knew that the job description in the application pack was vague. This had suited me at the time, as Tamsyn had said during the interviews that senior leadership roles were regularly rotated in order to play to each person's strengths and facilitate professional development. So it looked like the route to headship was already being mapped out. 'I want you to line-manage the new head of sixth, Heather Daulphin. I think you will get on well together. When can you meet her?' I was thinking that I had another term in my old job when Tamsyn told me:

> You'll do the timetable. I've found you a three-day course to go on in June; can you ask for time off to attend? And I want you to be in charge of the curriculum – it sort of goes with the timetable. I think you'd do a good job of staff cover. It needs someone who speaks as they find. I think that it will fit your Northern personality excellently. There will be other line management responsibilities of course, but we can discuss those later.

Many years later I would attend management courses and be introduced to the concept of distributed leadership. It was nothing new to me, as I had experienced it in full flow back in 1998.

It's a quirk of all school calendars that one of the first events of the year is an open evening for entry the following September. I was used to this and perfectly understood it to be an opportunity to market a school and ensure a full roll. Tamsyn announced to the newly reconstructed senior leadership team on the pink sofas that this year would be done differently:

> I want parents to see the school in operation. I'm proud of what we do, and we need parents to see this first-hand. The secret of a successful comprehensive school is to keep it fully comprehensive. We need a critical mass of bright middle-class students to help set a scholarly atmosphere that can only help students who don't have the same advantage. Middle-class parents have more choice; there is a thriving independent sector locally and selective schools just over the border in Barnet. We need to appeal to the middle

classes in order to give the best education to all students. A ghetto mentality will help no one.

I had rapidly become aware during my first few weeks that it was the mix of students that made Hampstead the unique school it was. The multinational component was there alright, and the school was popular with the children of academics from the colleges of London University in the south of the borough. Sons and daughters of visiting professors worked happily alongside the Children of the Storm. Word had clearly gone round some of the local embassies that Hampstead provided a superb, British, free education, so the daughter of the Slovak ambassador found herself in classes with children from the local council estate. The reputation of the school was not lost on New Labour MPs, who couldn't possibly be seen sending their children to independent or selective schools. None of this happened by accident. Tamsyn had spent the last 10 years developing this model of comprehensive education, creating and honing the true comprehensive, and she wasn't going to stop now:

> We will have a series of open mornings, every Wednesday, for the first half of this term. We'll take 50 parents each session, give them a school tour with a volunteer student guide, and take them back to the library for a short talk and a Q&A session. It'll be all over by break.

There was silence from the pink sofas. 'I'll run the first one, and you can watch me and then do one each.' So, with her educational version of the old surgeon's mantra: 'See one, do one, teach one', she had sorted our first half term.

Teaching at Hampstead was challenging but never boring. Tamsyn was alive with ideas for the senior team to try out. Shortly before the summer holidays she told me I was to run the sixth form induction course, called the History of Ideas, designed to get the students used to the sort of independent study they would need to master during their A levels and at university. 'It will need to cover the period from the Enlightenment to the present day – Heather will help you.'

This was useful, because Heather was a historian and I had no clue when the Enlightenment was. As Heather and I worked together on the programme and subsequently as very close colleagues, I began to see the logic of Tamsyn's leadership decisions. Heather and I had very different yet complementary skills. An imposing figure equally ascribed to both her north London upbringing and her Caribbean heritage in St Kitts, she had a unique ability to empathize with some of the most challenging students and bring about a love of history in even the most cynical of pupils. She had emotional intelligence in abundance and was the perfect antidote to my own emotional illiteracy. Her love of her subject rubbed off on all who came into contact with her. In many ways she embodied the Hampstead way, a colour-blind, class-unconscious determination that all students should achieve, regardless of their background. An ethos developed years before Ofsted's current focus on individual groups of students. There was no website support such as RAISEonline, little data, and negligible monitoring: it just happened. Personalized education, independent learning, and intervention strategies are all in the lexicon of twenty-first-century school improvement manuals, but at Hampstead in the 1990s it was simply a way of life.

As a head teacher in 2012, like many of my colleagues, I am aware that the job sometimes feels like building a house of cards. Successes achieved over several years can sometimes come tumbling down. Hard work and dedication can come to nothing by a small change in circumstances. A change in the intake of students, instability in the leadership of the school, staffing difficulties, or a less than favourable Ofsted inspection can all act as a catalyst for decline. The longer a head is in post, the more important it is to keep up fresh ideas and to strive towards continual improvement. Many successful heads have been caught out in the decade before retirement. Dame Tamsyn Imison knew this, and for 16 years she continued to improve Hampstead and was very much aware that there was always more to do. The job was never finished and would never be finished. Head teachers can't run schools by themselves; it's a team job. The best heads build the best teams and furnish those teams with passion, ideas, and trust, empowering them to work in the best interest of all students, to learn together and achieve together.

Glen Stevens

Mentor 2000–present

Currently inclusion manager

I have stayed long at Hampstead as a member of staff and now as a parent of two daughters who will be coming here because I know the school delivers across the board. My team of six mentors and I make a significant difference to many young people and their lives. Hampstead introduced counsellors and mentors in the 1990s, and even though finances are tight, it continues to increase the support given to this essential area. The school has a long history of caring for and valuing every child and member of staff. I know this because of the positive feedback we get from students and parents we have worked with. This continues long after they have left school.

Accessing learning is not easy for many of our students because they have complex needs. In 2012, as in the time of Tamsyn Imison's headship, a large number of children speak English as their second language (nearly 50 per cent), with around 50 different home languages. Out of 1,284 students, 458 are entitled to a free meal. This is usually their only hot meal of the day. We know that the school is for many their best refuge, and while we may look forward to the holidays, many of these students dread them. They may not have enough to eat, anywhere warm to stay, and no money to access the rich cultural life available to the more advantaged.

Our work is recognized by the Department for Education as well as the Achievement for All team who pay regular visits. Last week 30 Norwegian head teachers visited us, followed by a group of trainee heads, all of whom seemed impressed with the ways our children are supported. As a non-selective school with mixed attainment, Hampstead gives everybody a chance, and our expectations are the same for all, irrespective of background. We are very lucky that our own workforce reflects the students that we serve. The Macpherson Report (1999), which looked at the reasons for the murder of Stephen Lawrence, highlighted this as very important. The school now has a team of six mentors that I am proud to say reflects the wonderfully rich and diverse cultural backgrounds of our students. Two are former students from Hampstead. The younger members of our team are building the future 'Hampstead family'.

For those from war-torn countries the school is like a second home, providing nurturing and support. They need empathy and understanding. We are equipping students with the skills and strategies they need so their barriers to learning are identified and overcome.

My own and the team's learning is never-ending, and our teachers' learning is essential. Last Thursday another experienced teacher spent a day with me in order to learn to use our successful strategies for supporting vulnerable youngsters and managing behavioural issues. We are now supporting sexually vulnerable teenage girls who are at risk of underage sex and pregnancy. We also run two different parenting workshops, one run by a Somali worker for Somali parents. We are proud of our multi-agency work, and this means that no one is 'flying under the radar'. We also continue the tradition begun in the 1990s of involving the students themselves by using a group of trained peer mentors. They usually gain as much as those they are mentoring.

Phil Taylor

Teacher 1995–2002, director of IT, independent learning and new technologies, assistant head teacher

Currently course director, MA Education and Master's in Teaching and Learning, Birmingham City University

It's more to do with people and learning than technology

My interview for the post of director of information technology (IT) at Hampstead School may have begun a week or so before I first set foot in the building. I had been working in the IT Resources Library of the Institute of Education for about a year, but I was missing the buzz of school life. The job advertised at Hampstead offered an opportunity, too good to miss, to put into practice my developing views about the potential of information technology (as it was known before the 'c' of communication was added) as a tool for learning across the school curriculum. A young trainee teacher and I had a long discussion about using technology to enhance learning in English teaching. She was the daughter of the head of Hampstead. Our conversation may have whetted their appetite to see how I performed, especially in my mixed-ability class of governors that was part of the interview process!

Hampstead School was a thoroughly refreshing and exciting place to work. A relaxed atmosphere, no uniform, a diverse mix of youngsters, high expectations for achievement, and just one rule: be kind. The focus on learning for all, staff and students, permeated the school. We were all 'lead learners', exemplified by Tamsyn's own appetite for learning and her enthusiasm for others' learning. Daily interactions with students (as young people were always known at Hampstead) focused on their learning rather than the colour of their socks. Positive behaviour and attitudes were expected at all times, but individuality was encouraged over conformity. The school wanted students to think, reason, even challenge, which meant that 'because I say so' was an insufficient teacher exhortation. This taught me (and perhaps others too) a more mature, possibly harder, but undoubtedly better way to manage behaviour – through modelling, explanation, and sometimes negotiation.

In terms of my role, the school was committed to developing IT, independent learning, and new technologies, and was already investing heavily in resources and recognizing that this needed to be continued. My predecessors had begun to work with staff to integrate IT into subjects, and many teachers were experimenting with this relatively new resource. Some were less confident or did not see the potential benefits of adopting IT within their repertoire. Throughout my seven years at Hampstead, I followed four guiding principles for technology integration, which I set out at interview. These were entitlement, enhancement, access, and support. It is perhaps worth reflecting on these nearly 20 years on, to assess their continued relevance, or otherwise.

The introduction of the national curriculum in 1988 brought an 'entitlement' for all pupils to acquire 'IT capability' and to apply this within the contexts of their other subjects. This was a requirement that was not straightforward for schools to meet. Some chose to teach IT as a discrete subject, timetabled in time-honoured fashion. But a shortage of suitably trained teachers and limited access to resources were problematic. Computer rooms quickly became fully booked with IT lessons, usually just one a week or fortnight, with little or no availability for the second part of the national curriculum entitlement of application within subjects. With hindsight, it is staggering that a new curriculum subject was introduced by statute with seemingly little acknowledgement of the resource and teaching demands. An alternative to discrete IT was the cross-curricular approach adopted at Hampstead, whereby other subjects became the context for both acquisition and application of IT capability. This had a number of benefits, including that of potential subject enhancement and a greater incentive for teachers of other subjects to develop their own IT skills alongside their students, using real and relevant curriculum contexts. This avoided the manufacturing of scenarios for developing IT capability that could lack real purpose.

To implement cross-curricular IT the guiding principles of 'access' and 'support' were crucial. In the early days of computing in schools, limited and relatively expensive resources meant that access was the preserve of a small number of older students, often boys, who learnt programming techniques on computer science courses. When I started teaching, the BBC Micro was becoming a must-have resource for many teachers, widening access to increasing numbers of students through educationally designed software. Twenty-five years further on, schools are full of ICT, including complex networks, and I am writing these words on a smart phone! By the time I arrived at Hampstead networks were the norm, along with computer rooms of over 20 workstations, but portable technologies were emerging and expensive. I had started to experiment with networking in my previous school – the first server I managed had a 20 megabyte (yes, megabyte) hard disk, which we thought was massive and easily stored the necessary files. Today this would hold a couple of videos, if that. Networks brought wider and easier access to IT, despite the early challenge of serial cabling: if one link was broken, the whole network collapsed. However, limited workstations still meant that to resource a cross-curricular model properly, timetabled, discrete IT lessons had to be minimal. Many schools today have sufficient facilities to provide both discrete and cross-curricular experiences. Our approach was to enable open access, usually in computer rooms, which was complemented by satellite workstations and portable equipment. Teachers' use of interactive whiteboards was also encouraged, but it was no substitute for hands-on student interaction.

In terms of support, developing ICT activities always involved collaboration between the subject and ICT teams. This was a genuine two-way process – subject teachers brought a richness of curriculum ideas to the use of technology, while ICT specialists found practical ways to use ICT as a pedagogical tool. A common starting point was the identification of a subject topic that was hard to teach or difficult for students to grasp. So, for example, interest in Dickens' *Great Expectations* was raised by creating trailers for the David Lean film using available clips, and this led to increased skill in history too. We also tried to develop innovative and creative uses of ICT. For example, in a project with Year 6 children from feeder primaries combining art and music, pupils used graphics they created to generate complex rhythmic and percussive parts in music sequencing software. Then in groups they combined parts to produce and perform abstract 'industrial techno' pieces. When we played these at suitably high volume in assembly to the older students, their reaction was impressive and exciting.

Looking back, we made mistakes too. Like many schools at the time we were seduced by the claims of measurable learning gains made for expensive integrated learning systems. While some short-term benefits were apparent, most pupils quickly became bored with the repetitiveness, predictability, and simplistic rewards of the system, and research later showed that sustainable gains were not realized. Also, our early forays into hand-held computing revealed few useful educational applications, although this is of course different today. We learnt that ICT can sometimes get in the way, and this became a crucial test – ICT had to enhance, not interfere with, subject learning. The most successful uses of ICT were often the simplest: they involved the students in hands-on tasks and were rooted in real curriculum contexts and encouraged problem solving, thinking, and creativity. I was at Hampstead at a time when the internet was becoming accessible in schools, first through dial-up modems and later via our networks, and we were starting to see its potential for learning. Ten years on, I suspect that the educational possibilities afforded by the internet have yet to be fully realized. In particular, social networking is often an integral part of students' personal lives, but they do not always see its relevance to their formal learning.

Wherever possible subject and ICT teachers taught together, and I inherited and grew a brilliant team. We quickly learnt that ICT teachers needed to be technical, and technicians needed to be teaching assistants. We provided training and support for less ICT-confident teachers and gained, in return, valuable insights into different subject curricula and pedagogies. Some would argue this is expensive staffing – two to each class. But increasingly teachers gained enough confidence to use ICT independently with their classes, and ICT staff could work with others. In this way a developmental, capacity-building model grew, which was much more than coaching, because all parties benefited. The approach we developed was documented in two books: *IT: Every teacher's second subject?* (Taylor, 1997) and *Managing ICT in the Secondary School* (Imison and Taylor, 2001). The latter explored the institutional factors and school culture that support curriculum innovation, teacher development, and technology-enhanced learning.

I was fortunate to be involved in many other initiatives around and beyond ICT while at Hampstead. I played a part in the school's successful bid for Technology College status, resulting in my appointment as assistant head to lead the programme. While pursuing the expectation to enrich the specialist subjects, we kept a firm focus on cross-curricular ICT, so that the whole school benefited. Another key development during my time at Hampstead was the increasing use of assessment data to track and monitor students' progress, in part a response to increasing external drivers of performance such as league tables and inspection. I worked with others to develop our administrative systems to meet these new demands. With hindsight I fear this took me and others away from curriculum, pedagogical, and teacher development, and I doubt that this was a good trade-off. This is, I believe, the central challenge facing education today: to reconcile the competing demands on schools of quality, development, collaboration, innovation, and creativity on the one hand, and quality assurance, high-stakes assessment, and accountability on the other.

Many other influences on my future were nurtured at Hampstead, beyond the exceptional people who were my colleagues, including a fascination for education systems beyond the UK and a value of higher study. Involvement in a Comenius project allowed me to visit, collaborate with, and learn from practitioners in Norway, Belgium, and Denmark, and involved colleagues and students too. I have since built on this experience through various projects involving visits to Ukraine, Finland, Bulgaria, France, Portugal, and Turkey, each time challenging my assumptions about the way we do things and reinforcing the highly contextualized nature of all teaching and learning.

At Hampstead I was one of a group of teachers who had the amazing opportunity to participate in a school-based MA in School Development. This was run by Chris Watkins and Louise Stoll from the Institute of Education. They skilfully guided and challenged our thinking and enabled higher-level study, drawing on the growing research evidence base and linking it directly to our school. The MA provided a vehicle for my own professional growth and real collaborative development within the school, in many ways mirroring our approach to cross-curricular ICT. I have no doubt that the key to Hampstead's success was a culture of pupils, teachers, everyone as learners. Tamsyn modelled this through her own continual learning, demonstrated through her interest in all others' interests, and her regular reminders that 'you never arrive'. These varied experiences of collaborative professional learning at Hampstead have profoundly shaped my subsequent career, which has involved several consultancy, advisory, partnership, and academic tutoring roles. They inform a model for teacher development that I am currently progressing in my role as course director for the Master's in Teaching and Learning at Birmingham City University, as well as provide the focus for my own continued study.

When I left Hampstead to relocate to the Midlands, it was one of the hardest decisions of my career. I loved the school, its staff and pupils, and the opportunities it had given me. My next role as a key stage strategy consultant enabled me to pursue my interests in ICT, pedagogy, assessment, and teacher development on a larger scale. However, the early emphasis on discrete ICT teaching in what became the national strategies was, in my view, short-sighted. People seem to have varied experiences of the national strategies. For some they passed by unnoticed, and others remember them as prescriptive, or only for the 'three-part' lesson and the 'literacy hour'. As someone involved, at best I saw teachers responding eagerly to high-quality resources, co-produced by practitioners and specialists, underpinned by research evidence, and followed up in schools by teachers and consultants working in partnership. But I also saw the initial focus on collaborative teacher and school development overtaken by a creeping emphasis on judgemental observation and a deficit model of top-down improvement. This also infiltrated my later role as a school improvement partner (SIP), another national strategies initiative, which began as critical friendship to heads and governing bodies and became quasi-inspectorial. I suspect this was caused by a governmental requirement to show a measurable return on investment, so those tasked to support development were re-tasked to measure its impact. The latter tends to distort the former, in just the same way that high-stakes assessment encourages teaching to the test, and inspection fosters reductive formulae for 'good' and 'outstanding' practice.

What I am left with is that Hampstead, more than any other place I have worked, gave me the belief that teacher growth leads to learner growth, and ultimately to positive outcomes. It is people who matter more than technology, something we understood well at Hampstead, which was certainly a place where I was enabled to grow personally and professionally as one of many 'lead learners'. I am still a devout technophile, though in recent years this has taken second place to wider interests in teaching and learning, and creating the conditions, like those at Hampstead, where they can thrive.

Emma Wills

School counsellor 1990–present

Erik Erikson in *Identity and the Life Cycle* (1980) writes about our characteristics at the various stages of our development. He wrote that adolescence is not an affliction but a normative crisis. For me, the most sensitive vehicle for that normative process that happens in adolescence is the comprehensive school.

I joined Hampstead School in 1990 while training as a psychotherapist. After a conventional background and schooling, I left the London School of Economics determined not to be part of a world that identified a minority of students at the age of 11 as having a promising future, and labelled the majority 'failures', in a system set up in the 1940s. I therefore have to declare an early belief in the comprehensive movement, which came from those dedicated teachers and educationalists in many secondary modern schools who were proving that their students could achieve happiness and academic progress not expected of them. It was with delight that I found this philosophy in Hampstead School, an established comprehensive.

My own secondary schooling was first in a grammar and then a foundation school. I was very happy in both, and experienced some excellent teachers and some more modestly prepared for the demanding task of teaching. Demanding though teaching may be, much of the education of grammar and public school children comes from the expectations and support of home, particularly where books are read and loved; music is absorbed and made; art is appreciated and displayed; and high social values are cherished. My higher education was equally privileged, and I trained to teach in grammar schools, where I did not admire what I experienced. I chose to begin my teaching career in a secondary modern school established in the 1950s. There

I learnt from others what a dedicated staff could achieve with students who had failed the 11+ examination. The teaching enabled many of the students to overcome the expectation of failure and achieve results comparable to those of students in neighbouring grammar schools. Indeed, many parents chose that school for their successful 11+ sons and daughters, and it became more truly comprehensive, much to the annoyance of its then local member of Parliament.

After many years happily teaching, culminating in running a sixth form centre in a nearby successful comprehensive school, I retrained as a psychotherapist. This was a natural development from engagement with students and staff, when I often came away thinking that I might have offered wiser counsel, with better listening skills, had I been differently trained. While training I began part-time teaching at Hampstead School, where I found other perspectives on the comprehensive idea. These came mainly from the leadership of Tamsyn Imison, the extraordinary breadth of background of its students, and understanding that emerged from my new training. I found the school to be emotionally literate, and the staff nourished its young people equally with a strong sense of identity and an equality of worth.

Since completing training I have worked counselling teenagers. Erikson especially observes the preoccupation with self-image because 'we are most aware of our identity when we are just about to gain it' (Erikson, 1980: 27). The issue of knowing where one is going is paramount. Questions then arise about the characteristics that mark the truly comprehensive school and the characteristics of schools that may be damaging to students. Maslow urged people not to blindly repeat what they have done in the past, and this seems relevant to the objectives of many secretaries of state for education, who generally have experienced education not from their professional life and expertise but from their own schooling. It seems to me that this leads them to try to reproduce what they had. And it also seems the case that criticism of the comprehensive ideal is based upon unsound comparison between unselective comprehensive schools and those with selective entrance criteria, since a school cannot be 'comprehensive' if other schools within its area are selective.

In my current occupation I work with an integrative relational approach, which means that until I have formed a working relationship with a client, no progress will be made in coping or reparative work. An essential ingredient of this is unconditional respect for the client and what she or he is and brings. In a selective educational system there can be no starting point of equality, either of being valued or of opportunity. A truly comprehensive system offers the possibility of such a foundation, and that was what was approached in both the school where I began and Hampstead where I ended my teaching career, and where I began working therapeutically with students. I am dismayed at what I see to be an active return to the philosophy of the early post-war era, brave experiment though it may have been in its time, nearly a century ago.

Moira Young

Teacher 1974–2000, geography, head of year, teacher governor

Currently retired

In 1974, after five years in three different schools, I was teaching in a school with a delightful atmosphere, but I knew it was never going to be successful – a split site, few specialist classrooms, overcrowding, outside toilets and almost no playground. I had been living in Camden for some years, and Hampstead School was spoken of very highly and said to be a true comprehensive. In what I consider my best career move, I applied for and was appointed to the post of geography teacher. And I stayed for the next 27 years. My impression at the time was that as well as three geography classrooms with excellent resources, the whole site was light and airy. I was really impressed with the houserooms that were social areas for both staff and students and an internal telephone system whereby one could contact anyone in moments.

On an academic level I regard introducing residential field courses for the 16+ and A-level students as one of my major achievements. When I arrived in the school, we took out every class at least once a year on a day trip, but I believe the residential trip had major benefits in both the academic and social spheres. This activity was given a major boost when projects were made compulsory for all external examinations. I have to credit the ILEA, which gave grants to necessitous children and ran affordable field centres. Even though the old army huts with outdoor washing facilities and huge dormitories were quite a challenge, they certainly ensured that students from every background could spend five days in a different environment, bringing the dry old page to life and collaborating with one another and their teachers in a socially exciting manner. Later on, and unfortunately not long before they had to be sold owing to the break-up of the ILEA, renovations were made that made living conditions more comfortable. The loss of the affordable field centre is to be regretted, as the really needy could no longer have that great opportunity.

My other academic achievements were writing or updating courses across the year cohorts (and geography needs constant updating). There were the enjoyable times when as a department we would agree that change was needed, distribute tasks, and then hope to agree on the results. I must mention Giselle Winston, who was often truly inspired in this field. Then there were the horrors of adapting or changing material simply to suit a government diktat. Unforgettable was Education Secretary Ken Baker's decision to introduce the GCSE a year earlier than promised, with no extra resources and little in the way of teacher training.

Perhaps the best academic opportunity Hampstead gave me was to follow my main interests of climate, meteorology, and geomorphology by teaching these modules at A level. I really hope that my ex-students also think back to those days whenever climate change, pollution, and environmental degradation are at the top of the news and think, 'Yes, I know why that is happening'.

It was in 1984, with the appointment of Tamsyn, that the school was forced to look at itself, and underwent a sea change. Suddenly the head was seen – she might turn up anywhere! The children knew who she was; until that time they saw one of the senior management only if they were in trouble. Industrial unrest was at its height at this time – I remember changing my union when we were asked to go on strike in support of the miners. And who *was* this woman coming in and changing our cosy arrangements that were working so well? She removed the blinds in her office and put up curtains; she threw out the boardroom furniture and installed pink settees! She wanted to hear the children's points of view! Horror!

However, she was determined, and decided that from the following September the house system would be abolished and a year system introduced. At the time Hampstead was one of the few comprehensives that retained the house system. It certainly fostered a family atmosphere, but did not address the increasing academic recording burden, and there were too many crossed wires making the system inefficient. I was appointed head of fifth year (Year 11), and so was fortunate to continue supporting a cohort I knew well and was as fond of as any group I had ever taught. For the first time we had to devise and implement a pastoral curriculum that entailed careers and further education opportunities by keeping academic records, persuading students of the value of the National Record of Achievement (NRA), and creating modules for citizenship and sex education. One of my abiding memories is how tolerant the students were as we bumbled and grumbled our way through these new ideas. Luckily most of my tutors had taken their tutor groups for several years, and a trust had grown up between them. I had never had to work so closely with a team before, and our relationship was excellent throughout the year. It is certainly true that we had an academic oversight of our students that had never been collated in such a way before. It is also true that obtaining these records from some subject teachers was like getting blood from a stone. The year system thrived. I was fortunate in having such a stable tutor team and we moved together to Year 7 and took that cohort up to Year 11, as we did the next one. I can't stress too emphatically the importance of the input of tutors to the pastoral system. There is the experience from the different subject areas, a range of experiences acquired through background, age, and inspiration. At all times the students are of primary concern and, of course, the tutor is the first port of call for the parents, with whom good relations are vital.

A school is not all about classrooms and academics; it is part of the community. As a member of the PTA for many years, together with the brilliant history teacher and pillar of West Hampstead, Helene Bromnick, we went through the easy times when many mothers didn't work and could give plenty of time to activities, to the days when all women seemed to work full time. I really admired those parents who took part and played such an active part in fostering good relations with the school. We had many talented parents who had money-raising ideas, and the proceeds were used for extras for departments and helping children in a variety of ways.

Another pathway into the workings of a school is by being elected staff representative on the school governors. Apart from the awful ordeal of being on exclusion panels, the post gives one an insight into authority and government thinking but endows the privilege of being present at job interviews. The process of appointments at Hampstead was quite complex but fair. Rene Branton and Yvonne Sarch were the main instigators of a system that selected candidates for interview by using carefully selected criteria, and after the interviews often quite heated discussions took place. I think we appointed some excellent teachers to their posts.

When I left Hampstead School in 2000, the staff sang for me a song to a Beatles tune with words created by students on a field course. I remember the night before, thinking about making a witty speech, but I settled for very sincerely thanking the cleaners, the schoolkeepers, the secretarial staff, the parents, the teachers, and especially the students for making my life in the school so rewarding. We were all little cogs in a much bigger wheel.

Chapter 5
Context

Peter Mitchell

Director of education, Camden Local Education Authority, 1990–5

Former secondary head teacher in inner London, senior tutor responsible for the PGCE at the Institute of Education, University of London, chief inspector for Leicestershire LEA

Camden LEA: The early years and a postscript

This book is a celebration of a London inner-city comprehensive school. The purpose of this section is to explain more about the context within which Hampstead School once operated. It focuses on the early years of the new Camden Local Education Authority (1990–5), when much emphasis was placed on supporting local comprehensive schools. Hampstead School is on the edge of the London Borough of Camden, adjacent to the neighbouring borough of Brent. Its location is not to be confused with Hampstead, which borders the Heath. From its establishment in 1961, the school has enjoyed an enviable reputation as a mixed comprehensive school.

Until 1990 the ILEA managed all education in inner London. Despite its size – over 1,000 primary and 150 secondary schools – ILEA provided local support through its divisions, which usually covered one or two boroughs. At the same time management from County Hall ensured that services were unified. Particularly noteworthy was the commitment of ILEA to comprehensive education. From the mid-1970s, when the last of the inner-city grammar schools closed, secondary schools could expect more balanced (comprehensive) intakes across inner London. Prior to that decision many inner-London schools were in fact secondary modern schools running alongside grammar schools.

The demise of ILEA owed much to the political climate of the 1980s. It was seen as a high-spending education authority. In 1986 came the break-up of the Greater London Council, and ILEA followed a similar fate in 1990. In 1988, in anticipation of this change, 13 inner London boroughs began preparations for taking over education from ILEA. Members (councillors) and officers in the boroughs had little or no experience of managing an education service. To be successful, members had to value integrating a universal service with more focused services.

The Borough of Camden is deceptive to the outsider. It seems to resonate with names – Hampstead, Highgate, Holborn, and St Pancras – that conjure up a picture of settled private and business success. In fact, Camden exemplifies one of the characteristics of inner London: because there has never been a master plan for London it has, unlike Paris, grown haphazardly. Camden is a mixture of social and ethnic backgrounds. Its comprehensive schools reflect this mixture. Hampstead School had an intake from across the diverse population of its immediate environs.

The year 1990 was not an ideal time to establish a new Local Education Authority. The national economy was going through a difficult period, and the explicit purpose of breaking up ILEA was to reduce the cost of running education in inner London. ILEA officers provided briefing papers for the boroughs, but these only gave an estimate of the budget required to run the new devolved service. From the start Camden set out to articulate a vision and values for the new service, which would help to give unity of purpose to the new authority. This vision was built around the comprehensive principle developed by Pat Daunt in his seminal work *Comprehensive Values*, namely, 'All students are of equal worth'.

A commitment to community education and, therefore, lifelong learning was also a key part of the vision. The beginning of comprehensive schools in the 1960s saw only modest attempts to understand how curriculum and learning should be organized in a non-selective school. The emphasis was almost entirely on how to structure the education service rather than on the content of lessons. Underpinning the notion of equal worth is the belief that all children are capable of learning as long as lessons are differentiated to meet their individual needs. Support for comprehensive education was thus put at the heart of the new Camden LEA. Apart from the obvious distinction between schools on the basis of gender and religion, schools remained non-selective.

An emphasis on community education, and therefore lifelong learning, provided a basis for making adult, youth, and further education part of the new unified service. By making community education part of the stated purpose of Camden LEA, we were emphasizing the importance of preparing young people for learning beyond school and compulsory education.

Appointing a full department of staff in one year was difficult. There was much speculation about how the boroughs would cope with the additional demands on their services. ILEA, probably tongue in cheek, predicted the new LEAs would fail to pay the teachers on time and provide sufficient taxis to pick up the children with special needs. More seriously, the *London Evening Standard* predicted that Camden, out of the 13 new LEAs, would find it most difficult to hold onto its secondary schools. This was at the height of the government's push to encourage secondary schools to opt out of local authority control. The newspaper was predicting that the confident secondary schools in Camden would not welcome being managed by an authority that was caricatured as being on the 'loony left' end of the political spectrum.

In the circumstances it was obvious that Camden Borough had to be credible and to build confidence with the schools from day one. Having a clear vision was an important starting point. The new authority knew, however, that it would be judged by the clarity and efficiency of its services. These services would partly be provided by central council services such as payroll and information technology. We were fortunate to be part of a borough council making a steady transformation into what would be recognized as one of the most caring and efficient local government authorities in the country. The new education department made an important contribution to this transformation and provided the majority of the services for schools.

Establishing a new department from scratch meant we were able to look for a commitment to working specifically in education. This particularly applied to officers engaged in resource management, who could have pursued careers in any of the other borough departments or indeed in the private sector. It was notably encouraging to schools to be served by officers with a wide interest in education. The location of Camden meant we were able to recruit from outer London boroughs as well as ex-ILEA employees. The former had the priceless asset of being familiar with working in a small LEA. These appointments were being made at a time when schools were taking more responsibility for managing devolved budgets. From the beginning Camden was aware it had to make services attractive to schools, otherwise they might buy them elsewhere. It is sometimes forgotten that ILEA had introduced the idea of devolved budgets as far back as the late 1970s. The Alternative Use of Resources Scheme gave schools the opportunity to spend part of their annual budget on whatever was a priority for the school, while the allocation of basic staffing was controlled centrally.

The management of schools can be divided into two parts: the executive and the professional. The former focuses on resource management and the latter on teaching and learning. The new Camden LEA replicated this structure. The appointment of a strong inspectorate, covering all the major disciplines of the curriculum, was a clear statement of intent. We had inherited some of the most admired and successful schools in London, and understood that being a credible LEA would depend on gaining their immediate respect.

Inspectors are the staff who work most directly with teachers. The new LEA's support for comprehensive school values and principles was transmitted to schools through the relationships that inspectors and officers established with schools. Each school had a named inspector who provided the school's main link with the education department. In addition they supported teaching and learning in their discipline across all the schools. An annual programme of inspections ensured standards were monitored.

Inspectors presented reports to the school, parents, and governors. They also presented reports formally at meetings of the education committee. It was important that the local community understand each school in some depth. Local councillors would expect to be involved in the follow-up to an inspection. A local authority inspection team has the advantage, over one based nationally, of identifying weaknesses and continuing to work closely with the school in the post-inspection period. The team can also draw on local knowledge held by other departments of the local authority. They are in a strong position to network schools, bringing about the exchange of ideas that aim to support school improvement. Successive governments have consistently undervalued the importance of knowledge held by democratically elected local government institutions.

The inspection team was supported by officers carrying out annual statistical reviews of the performance of each school. These reviews formed the basis for wide-ranging debates: both internal school debates and debates with inspectors and officers. We were focused on providing support for teachers, as it is work in classrooms that drives up the performance of children and young people. This is often overlooked in all the debates about the structure of education.

The link inspector for Hampstead during the 1990s writes about his experience of working with the school and more widely in the LEA:

Hampstead was known (in the 1990s) for its innovation, creativity, and boldness. It embraced new initiatives from the government and the LEA, and used them to further its own high level aims. Adoption of an initiative always followed fierce debate among staff, governors, and sometimes pupils about how the initiative could contribute to raising standards.

The school's strong independent spirit sometimes brought it into conflict with the LEA. We deployed experienced officers and inspectors to link with the school. The partnership established was positive and challenging.

At the same time as supporting individual schools the LEA provided leadership on behalf of all the communities in Camden. With its thorough knowledge and understanding of the strengths and weaknesses of all schools, the LEA was able to facilitate the sharing of good practice across schools. Senior staff at Hampstead made significant contributions to the improvement of other secondary schools in the area through in-service training, mentoring, and the generous sharing of good practice.

(Grant, 2012)

Hampstead School was able to set its strong sense of its own identity alongside a commitment to working closely with the education department. It was an integral part of the new LEA. By working so closely with officers and inspectors, the school contributed to the successful establishment of Camden as an education authority.

The importance attached to support for teaching and learning was exemplified by the position of the Education Development Centre (EDC), which was deliberately located within the education department. The head of the EDC, reflecting on taking over from ILEA, noted the need to change staff development practices:

There was a need to change the approach by moving to the provision of high quality training and development opportunities that balanced the needs of schools and individuals; that set out the notion of entitlement and equality of access for teachers, support staff and governors, and demonstrated the link between professional development and school improvement. Placing the EDC within the education department gave a clear message about the importance of staff development for improving the learning of children and young people. The central position of the EDC helped to create the respect and trust which underpins the school/training partnerships established in Camden. Meetings for all stakeholders in the LEA were held in the EDC, thus ensuring a widespread appreciation of the work of the centre. [This is] a stark contrast with the position where professional development is isolated from the mainstream debates in education. Good teaching is at the heart of school improvement. Camden's emphasis on support for learning permeated the work of all departments in the new LEA. The EDC gave unity and coherence to this support.

(Tilbrook, 2012)

The morale of schools and parents is very much bound up with the intake of schools. The number of first-choice pupils is an indicator of how parents feel about a school. Parents who feel positive they have made the correct choice for their child are much more likely to support the school. Camden's admissions policy encouraged parents to look first at their local school. If parents see this as the starting point for making their choice of school, then there is more likely to be strong support for local schools. This support strengthens links between primary and secondary schools. When the opposite is the case and parents are encouraged to exercise choice over a wide area, many children will be forced to travel outside their local area. This makes links between parents and schools more tenuous and difficult to sustain. Governments that put choice at the centre of education policy are making it more difficult for parents to work with schools to support their children's education.

Camden is fortunate to have many parents willing to work for the improvement of children's learning across all abilities and backgrounds. They support comprehensive education, even though many could choose to pay for private education. The schools have benefited greatly from parental support. Because of the nature of borough boundaries and the sound reputation of Camden's schools, there has been a long tradition of Camden educating children and young people from neighbouring boroughs – it is the nature of the inner city that makes it possible for a school to be the local school for children from more than one LEA. Hampstead is a case in point: many pupils from Brent have been educated at Hampstead School. The school would be the first to acknowledge that this brought many well-motivated children and parents into the school. The contrast with the situation in many other local authorities in London is striking, where the absence of commitment to state-run comprehensive education by many middle-class parents leaves some schools struggling to gain support from their community.

Setting up a new LEA in a local authority where many parents and community groups were prepared to work with the authority meant establishing structures that encouraged participation and supported consultation. This particularly applied to decision making about key education policies. The political context brought teachers and governors into contact with members. The chair of education quickly made himself familiar with the character of the education service Camden had inherited. Clear structures and procedure to support consultation were established. Head teachers,

teachers, parents, governors, and members were at the heart of this process. Schools were seen as an integral part of the management of the LEA. As such they were in a position to act in partnership with those members who took important decisions affecting, for example, the resourcing of schools. Any idea that members and officers in Camden took important decisions without the involvement of schools and their representatives would be far from the truth. Successive governments have reduced the responsibilities of LEAs. This has weakened the pool of people willing to become local councillors. Why become a local councillor when your ability to support local schools is being systematically eroded?

In addition to consulting schools, meetings were held with other key stakeholders. The inspector responsible for careers and post-16 education established regular meetings with representatives from local industry, commerce, and further and higher education. The LEA is in a position to nurture links between schools and the wider community. These links keep teachers up to date with the expectations on their students when they leave school. Forums were established to address the interests of minority groups in Camden: there is, for example, a strong Somali community that needed support; alternative schools for Afro-Caribbean pupils, in the evenings and weekends, also had their own forum. These forums provided feedback on the experience of ethnic minorities in mainstream schools. The notion of a comprehensive education service is built firmly around the work of schools. The partnerships and networks we established extended the idea across all ages and social and ethnic backgrounds. Supporting individuals and groups from across the community was an important way of emphasizing how the principle of equal worth pervades the work of the LEA.

The first five years of the new LEA ensured the schools operated in a stable environment. During this period two secondary schools did opt out of local authority control. One did so because it wished to move out of the borough to be nearer the main concentration of its intake in outer London; the other opted out because its religious order wished to take full advantage of the financial incentives being offered by the government. The borough accepted its new responsibilities with growing confidence. Early years education was moved from social services to education, with emphasis being placed on the value of continuity to a child's education. A performing arts centre was established that became the home for Camden's youth orchestra. This is an example of the type of activity, provided by an LEA, that is beyond the means of an individual school.

The explicit emphasis on supporting comprehensive primary and secondary schools provided a context where schools felt valued. Camden had inherited some of the strongest schools in inner London. This meant that the new education department had to be prepared to challenge schools that were well respected in their local community and had to make some difficult decisions. We had, for example, to close three of the schools we inherited. There was insufficient support for two of the special schools – one a boarding school and one a poorly performing secondary school that had insufficient pupils.

There have been two particularly significant local developments since the LEA was established. In 2003 the London Challenge was launched. Although the Challenge focused on boroughs other than Camden, its success made it of more general significance. It set out to break the link between disadvantage and low achievement. The fact that London's schools now perform above the national average is an indication of how successful it has been. Social and economic factors obviously play a significant part in some children's underperformance; it is also widely acknowledged that good teaching nurtured by support systems, which build the confidence of teachers, can help their pupils overcome their disadvantages. The London Challenge recognized this and made support for teachers the basis on which standards improved. It also sought to widen the commitment to raising standards by seeking to fully engage communities in improving schools.

For Camden the most significant development has been a review of the education service in the borough. The report of the Camden Education Commission was published in 2011, 21 years after Camden LEA was established. The present government's academy programme, and the encouragement of free schools, made it timely to review and plan the future of education in the borough. The present government believes that freedom from LEA control will help to raise standards. This view fails to acknowledge how much freedom and support schools have when they remain within the LEA. It is certainly questionable whether more freedom will produce more school improvement; the Programme for International Student Assessment (PISA) has recently questioned whether schools in England need more freedom (2011).

At the heart of the commission's proposals is the Camden Partnership for Education Excellence (CPEE), which has the core aim of ensuring that all schools move from good to outstanding. Where schools have a good reputation, there is always the possibility that they will assume there is small room for improvement, and coasting can become the norm. Camden Council will work with partners – schools – through the CPEE to encourage bottom-up collaboration and challenging targets that are agreed by the partners. The management board of the CPEE will include lead members and lead officers from the council. Significantly for the status of the CPEE, one of the lead officers will be the chief executive of the council. Residents and outside visitors to the borough will be left in no doubt about the importance attached to the quality of learning in Camden schools.

The council, as the single democratically accountable body, will continue to give strategic leadership to education in the borough. It will work to the comprehensive principle of equal worth by promoting the interests of all young people and supporting high standards for all. Academies and free schools can become members of the CPEE so long as they follow Camden's admissions code and participate in behaviour and attendance partnerships.

Looking back to where Camden LEA started, the CPEE represents a shift in emphasis towards local policy making being driven by schools, including governors, teachers, and parents. The collective experiences of these groups will show where policy priorities should lie.

If comprehensive education is to continue to promote the learning of all children and young people, other LEAs will need to build partnerships similar to the CPEE. There is evidence that some LEAs have been so disheartened by the continual erosion of their role in local education that they have literally withdrawn from all but the minority of statutory services they continue to run. Some academies have formed chains (partnerships) outside the local LEA. It is difficult to see how these will compare with the CPEE being established in Camden. Camden's proposal will link schools to local government, local business, local stakeholder groups, and voluntary groups, while at the same time respecting the importance of policy leadership coming from the schools.

The future of LEAs lies in the kind of strategic role and partnerships being developed in Camden. If schools choose to ignore the opportunities presented by local partnerships involving the LEA, then non-selective education, of the kind so well represented by Hampstead School, will be seriously at risk. Already it is common to distinguish academies and free schools, accountable to the secretary of state, from comprehensive schools. Are we to assume that these new forms of school organization are free to be selective? That really would distinguish them from comprehensive schools. The success of schools in Camden should be based upon local schools being committed to a comprehensive provision across the whole borough.

Peter Newsam

Chief education officer for the Inner London Education Authority 1975–81, chairman of the Commission for Racial Equality, 1981–5, director of the Institute of Education, University of London, 1989–94, chief schools adjudicator, 1999–2002

Hampstead School in the ILEA

BACKGROUND AND CONTEXT

In 1980 Hampstead School was a comprehensive secondary school maintained by the ILEA. Before 1947 London had secondary schools attended by a small proportion of its children, and elementary schools attended by the rest. The 1947 *London School Plan* outlined how comprehensive schools were designed to provide secondary education for all between the ages of 11 and 18, admitting children of all abilities and aptitudes. In a speech to head teachers in 1947, the local authority's chief inspector of schools defined the nature of these schools:

> The comprehensive schools will be integrated communities providing social life and a very large element of classroom education common to all. The schools will in fact help to spread a common culture, a culture that will enrich the lives of everybody, and to some extent be independent of the kind of work people do or the incomes they earn. The comprehensive high schools will not, however, ignore the vocational interests of their pupils. It will be necessary for them to do everything possible to safeguard the high academic standards now associated with the old-established secondary schools, for on these depends the recruitment to our professions. Equally necessary will be the development of advanced vocational courses, and comprehensive high schools may be expected to develop technical and commercial as well as academic subjects, each at sixth form level, reaching an advanced standard and exerting a bracing influence on the work of other parts of the school. The uncommon man with high academic or practical aptitudes will not be neglected.
>
> (Savage, 1947)

As comprehensive schools were to include children of all aptitudes and abilities, they needed a curriculum wide enough to meet those needs within each school, rather than as in the past following selection at age 11, within different types of school. The plan aspired to the aim that comprehensive schools should enable 'in time a healthy mutual regard and understanding between persons of different kinds of ability with far-reaching effects on the cultural, industrial, and commercial life of the nation and the social life of its people'.

In the following years some fifty of London's 220 secondary schools – Hampstead was one – were developed as comprehensives, but by the early 1970s there were still 45 schools selecting children at age 11. This meant that it was impossible for most other secondary schools to be fully comprehensive, in the sense of admitting a balanced intake of children of all abilities. In 1977 selection in all publicly funded schools in London ended, but the problem of creating schools that are fully comprehensive remains to this day. Every year London's selective independent schools admit up to 10 per cent of the age group.

THE ILEA's FUNCTIONS

The separate functions of the ILEA and secondary schools in London were legally established and well understood by each. The ILEA's main functions were set out in the 1960 Royal Commission on the Government of London and included control and management of capital programmes. In terms of capital costs the ILEA, and the London County Council before it, bought sites for schools and provided the buildings, with capital funds authorized by central government – over time acquired and repaid from the ILEA's revenue budget. Other functions were year-by-year management of the revenue budget; control over the disposition and organization of educational institutions; central negotiations with teachers; organization of major central resources; and management of further and higher education, and adult and special education. A variety of other services were provided that individual schools found difficult or impossible to provide themselves, including a careers service; a youth service operating in evenings and holiday periods; and notably, access to a London-wide orchestra and theatres managed by the ILEA.

Other functions not specifically mentioned by the Royal Commission were provided for in legislation and included decisions on the number of teachers the authority could employ and their equitable distribution; managing school admissions and ensuring sufficient school places for all children; keeping records of school attendance; and ensuring parental compliance with their duty in this regard. Finally, the authority had to satisfy the legislative requirement that the education provided was 'efficient' and not 'at unreasonable public expense'. In carrying out these functions the ILEA employed divisional officers in each of its 10 divisions. In addition, local and London-wide inspectors were employed who were to assist schools to meet the requirements of efficient education and to inform the ILEA, through school visits or other forms of inspection, how the school system was working and what was needed to help individual schools function better.

The internal organization and management of secondary schools, in London and elsewhere, were set out in *Instruments and Articles of Government*. Nationally, these were in standard form, with only minor variations. They had been approved by the secretary of state and could not be altered without his permission either by a school or by the ILEA. Between them, the *Instruments and Articles of Government* laid down such matters as the composition of the school's governing body, responsibility for the curriculum, and the relative responsibilities of the school governors and the head teacher. The internal workings of any school were a matter for a school's governors and the head teacher to determine. The functions of the ILEA did not include any right to control those internal arrangements.

VALUES AND COMPREHENSIVE EDUCATION
London's general approach to the nature and purpose of a comprehensive school had not radically changed between 1947 and 1980. What had changed, both nationally and in some quarters of London, was a largely undisputed acceptance of the values expressed in the *London School Plan*. Sharp differences of opinion developed. Public debate about the merits of comprehensive schools was increasingly led by people, including elements of the national press, who had only second-hand or fleeting experience of the schools. The main argument that now developed started from the assumption that as it was obvious that different children had different needs, it was natural that they should be educated in separate institutions. In the minds of some politicians and elements of the press, placing all children together was an act of social engineering. Placing children in separate institutions was not perceived as social engineering but as uncontested. Accompanied by the belief that the purpose of education was to establish and then concentrate on the differences between children, defined by the results of tests with right or wrong answers, it was argued that those who did not see that the purpose of education was to establish differences between children must therefore believe that such differences were unimportant and should be ignored. It was argued therefore that the effect of teaching all children in the same school would be to retard the proper education of clever children. A reading of the *London School Plan,* in particular the extract quoted on p. 142, would

have shown that this was a total misunderstanding of the nature of a comprehensive school.

It was not the role of the ILEA, as a public authority, to tell teachers or school governors what to think, but it did appear necessary to repeat the principles on which it had been working since 1947. As ILEA education officer in a speech to head teachers in 1979, I dealt with two issues. The first concerned the bad-tempered and often wildly inaccurate arguments about secondary education that were taking place:

> I hope we will be able to raise the level of debate over the next year or so. Initially, perhaps, by refraining from exclusive reliance on either/or types of argument and working on some that say 'both'. That would prevent people either supposing that the principal aim of education is to sort, give marks to, or concentrate on the differences between children, or from veering to the other extreme of insisting that it is only what children have or can undertake in common that is permissible. It is surely obvious that we must hold both ideas in our heads at the same time. Individual differences between children are important. Any school must recognize this. But a school should not concentrate exclusively on what separates one individual from another. Children pursuing individual programmes with head-sets on would constitute a solipsistic nightmare. Heads need to create conditions under which there can be a conscious and sensitive exploration of what the young have in common, as human beings and future citizens. This has nothing much to do with intelligence or skill in passing examinations.

The second issue I raised was a reminder of what the government of the day had recognized in 1970, when what had been described as 'severely subnormal children' became the responsibility of education authorities rather than health authorities. The principle underlying that change in responsibilities was that all children at some level can learn. That principle was not new. It had been long established with particular clarity in 1869, by the Reverend Edward Thring, then a distinguished headmaster of Uppingham School. 'There is a path', Thring had declared, 'which all must tread … Some move quicker than others, some more slowly; but all can move. All can walk part of the way with genius'. The principle embodied in that final sentence defines an important element of what a comprehensive school is. A comprehensive school promotes inclusion. It is opposed to social or educational exclusion of any kind.

Over the 30 years since 1980, the problem of low-grade thinking about education and the poor quality of public and parliamentary debate about it has become increasingly serious. There are several reasons why this has happened. One is that, since 1997, no prime minister has attended, taught in, or had any responsibility as a school governor or member of an education committee for any publicly funded school in England before assuming ultimate political control of all of this country's schools. Unfortunately, once appointed, none has displayed in speech or deed anything other than superficial understanding of the systems that in the name of reform they have been busy (or allowed others to become busy) dismantling or mismanaging at huge public expense. In these circumstances, it has become increasingly necessary for comprehensive schools to hold their nerve and retain their values. It is greatly to its credit that this is what Hampstead School has consistently managed to do.

Chris Watkins

Institute of Education, University of London. Head of academic group – assessment, guidance, and effective learning 1995–2000, MA course leader 1992–2005; reader in education 2000–present

'Not papering over the cracks': Learning from a school-based MA at Hampstead School

I first experienced Hampstead School in 1975. I was new to London, and a friend through other circles, Chris Robertson, enabled me to talk with some young people about research I was doing into adolescents' perceptions of social episodes. So I found myself walking along Westbere Road one morning with pupils arriving at school, and as I went in and found my way around, I immediately had a feeling I have in a small number of schools: I felt at home. Having been a teacher in a comprehensive school in Kent – the only comprehensive school in Kent – I was used to crowdedness and busyness, but here there was a great sense of engaged activity and connectedness.

Waiting outside the deputy head's office, I noticed that any student who was late to school was asked to report to her office, or if she was unavailable, to write up their reasons for lateness. It made interesting reading, including gems such as 'Abducted by aliens' – a foretaste of the creative communication to come!

As the next couple of decades went by I continued to meet teachers from Hampstead School at a range of meetings and conferences that were commonplace in London teachers' lives in those days, such as Saturday conferences where 200 teachers turned up to discuss such things as personal-social education and the national curriculum. Hampstead teachers usually struck me as engaged and active professionals with a real commitment to make schooling an important aspect of young people's lives. Such commitment was not always a feature of the teachers I was meeting in other schools.

So when in 1997 the possibility arose of working with my colleague Louise Stoll to run a school-based Master's degree at Hampstead, I was keen. October 1997 saw a whole-school inset day to introduce the programme and invite teachers to join. In negotiation with the senior colleagues in the school, the theme was not the usual 'training' by outsiders that such days have mostly become. Its title was Future Schools and How to Get There From Here, with staff working in differently composed groups through the day. After a presentation on predictions about the future, staff were invited to say which three they would fight for and which three they would fight against. Then the conversation moved to school, supported by the results of a just-completed staff survey on key themes in school effectiveness. The highest level of agreement was with these two items: 'If staff have problems with their teaching they are likely to turn to colleagues for help', and 'Staff encourage pupils to try their very best.' These struck me as affirming evidence of the school's culture. Perhaps more important was the fact that when staff were asked to respond to the same questionnaire items in terms of rating their importance for a school to be effective, three items received almost unanimous support: 'The primary concern of everyone in the school is pupil learning', 'Teachers in this school make efforts to learn from their own practice', and 'Teachers in this school believe that all pupils can learn'. The potential that derived from such an explicit focus on learning excited me, and my own earlier impressions of Hampstead staff were affirmed by the fact that a majority of them agreed with the statement, 'I feel I am making a significant difference to the lives of my pupils'.

Staff comments in the questionnaire also highlighted the high energy level of the school at that time through comments such as, 'We've seen more pilots than British Airways'. But a thoughtful resolution to a time of multiple initiatives was also reflected in comments such as, 'We must replace bandwagons with successful innovations to avoid the unnecessary overload'. With this start, 14 colleagues began the core module, which was designed to address issues of understanding learning and teaching and then go on to examine how change may be promoted. After-school sessions in the staffroom saw the group involved in addressing active collaborative learning in an active collaborative way. Brief presentations, reading, and discussion took us into all the key areas. And very soon it was clear that these busy teachers were prepared to stretch themselves in thinking and practice. On occasions when I might refer to a particular text and ask whether anyone was interested to read it, there were always more requests than copies. This was not my experience in other schools.

As the meetings went on it became clearer that participants were seeking to learn deeply, and they chose to address such issues as the quality of learning in classrooms, departments, and whole school; how matters of creativity and motivation were handled; and an examination of what dynamics explained the small number of disaffected teachers who did not engage in a learning culture.

The following term saw us addressing change, leading to colleagues proposing how change should best be handled in the school contexts they knew and worked in. After completing other modules at the IOE, the MA was completed by dissertation. These addressed and investigated a rich range of key issues, including pupil grouping, using ICT to improve learning, gender patterns in mathematics, disaffected pupils, and so on. The school carried out its own evaluation, which highlighted that 'participants feel they have derived considerable personal professional benefits from the MA, in particular the core module, the way it was taught and its impact on teaching and learning'.

Because school-based Master's degrees were an unusual form of provision at the IOE, we engaged the services of an external evaluator. The report included: 'Teachers were unanimous in endorsing the MA in School Development, despite initial administrative hitches and some anxiety about the additional work'. One of the significant comments about the MA in relation to the school was: 'Schools that wanted to paper over the cracks wouldn't do it'. Respondents agreed that 'Staff who were not participating in the course should be kept in touch with the programme and its outcomes, so as to involve as many people as possible in facing future challenges'.

The course could even have had impact beyond the school, with some of the group creating their own publications (Sullivan, 2000; Rayner, 1999), and – dare I suggest – one of them leading similar provision of a Master's in Teaching and Learning in what may be a similar style.

So my first impressions with pupils were affirmed and extended with staff: that a socially active and engaging, communicative environment can also be one in which our key educational goals can be achieved. In today's terms it has been shown that few educational systems achieve both equity and excellence. The key element of classroom and school effects is their culture, and here I saw a culture for achieving both. I saw that the school was run as an organization for learning and making a difference, rather than the corporate style that has been growing in secondary schools more recently and in some cases has led to the regression of schooling to an authoritarian past. The staff at all levels were engaged with thinking about the future, and there was very little divisive talk, the sort that puts people – students or teachers – into categories and stops there. Certainly differences were noted and talked about, but in a way that sought to understand and address them for the greater good. Whether it related to disaffected staff or students, I found the people I worked with wanted to understand better in order to improve matters. And it seems significant that I can hardly remember any talk of 'ability', or the dominant classroom practices that utilize this hypothetical term.

My experience at the school affirmed my belief that committed teachers in demanding contexts are prepared to stretch themselves even further, if they are treated to a collaborative inquiry-based culture. In 1997 there had already been years of the 'discourse of derision' (Ball, 1990), which government used against teachers and schools. But Hampstead teachers were prepared to be resilient in the face of this and to continue to follow high-level educational goals. I left with a strengthened conviction that schools that focus on learning make the biggest difference to students' lives. At about the same time as co-leading the MA in Hampstead, I founded the Institute-based MA in Effective Learning. This was in part a response to the post-national curriculum world, in which it became impossible to maintain courses in pastoral care and personal–social education, and my colleagues and I resolved to address the core matter that had motivated us: learning, in a rich and human sense. My years leading the MA in Effective Learning were a brilliant experience, with teachers from London schools transforming – and I do not use that word easily – the culture of learning in their classrooms (see some examples in Watkins, 2005). But they reported this as being an increasingly difficult job: in schools other than Hampstead, the context was not helping. So in 2005 I resigned my full-time post in order to work more with the contexts and dynamics that were affecting learning, and since then have been leading projects to support the development of learning-centred classrooms and schools in a range of places across England.

One of the peculiar things about schools is that in most of them, learning is rarely discussed (Watkins, 2003). Increasingly the talk about 'performance' in terms of grades and levels has forced out a focus on learning, even more so than the previous (and returning) focus on teaching. Yet the research evidence demonstrates that a focus on learning can enhance performance in learning and achievement in tests and examinations, while a focus on performance alone can actually inhibit these achievements, for a number of reasons related to how people learn (Watkins, 2010). This evidence contradicts what has become known as 'the state theory of learning' in England: the idea that a combination of the repeated high-stakes testing of pupils, a national curriculum, and mandated pedagogy in numeracy and literacy will raise 'standards' (Balarin and Lauder, 2009).

The value of a developed focus on learning emerges as a finding in research, and more recently at international level as a hallmark of the top-performing countries such as Finland. It is increasingly hard to find in England's secondary schools. Examples such as Mathew Moss School in Rochdale or Bay View School in Gosport offer inspiring experiences, but the overall picture has changed as a result of successive governments adopting a pressurizing role, alongside a narrowing of educational goals to the achievement of grades in public examinations. The dynamics of fear (Galton and MacBeath, 2008) that I now experience affecting schools in England was not in evidence in Hampstead School.

My own learning has involved me and my colleagues spending a number of years on how best to organize decades of research and understanding about learning in classrooms (Watkins *et al.,* 2007). Our core headings were: active learning, collaborative learning, learner-driven learning, and learning about learning. These four apply equally to teachers' learning.

John Ashworth

Then director of the London School of Economics, later director of the British Library

Memories of teaching on the History of Ideas: Sixth form induction programme at Hampstead School 1994–8

Walking into a classroom at Hampstead School to talk about science, technology, and industry was a pretty daunting experience for someone like me, used to teaching at a university: many more students than chairs; belongings, books, and coats everywhere, and a slightly raucous hubbub. I always had a joke of some sort ready to attract their attention and called for volunteers (always the boys, I pointed out) to operate my slide projector – no PowerPoint in those days. My task was to help the sixth form see how they might relate their academic studies to a bigger or more comprehensive picture. I usually chose to start with a couple of topics, one contemporary (such as should we build more nuclear power stations or should the government subsidize IT start-ups) and one historical (such as why were the scientific insights of the Greeks not followed up in the Middle Ages, or were the Dark Ages really dark), which illustrated the connections between science, technology, and society. I never needed more than a couple of topics, because the students' questions and interruptions rapidly generated a discussion that led us into the most unexpected areas. I remember trying to deal with the importance of the concept of zero in mathematics and book-keeping that severely taxed my competence, and a fascinating discussion of the nature and importance of cosmetics in ancient Rome that really caught the attention of the girls. We always seemed to run out of time but never out of questions, and they were without a doubt the liveliest audience I have ever had. It was always great fun, certainly for me, and I'm pretty sure for them.

Chapter 6

Postscript

Tamsyn Imison

Hampstead School in the last two decades of the twentieth century steadily improved to become one of the many higher achieving comprehensives in the country, as its Ofsted inspections showed. Its success was surprising for some people because it did not conform to the norms expected of a 'good' school. There was no uniform, no bells or tannoys. Both staff and students were expected to focus on both their own and others' learning, and learning was an active and enjoyable process for the majority. Our assemblies were appropriate for our multicultural intake where respect, consideration, and valuing others were our priority. For us, spiritual values were not just a matter of religious ritual. We were at the forefront of using data analysis and action research to develop and support learning, but these were still early days. In the 13 years that have elapsed since 2000, all schools now use these important tools to ensure that their student cohorts are high achievers. Our 50 per cent of students achieving five A–C grades is more like 80–90 per cent in most comprehensives, including Hampstead, in 2013. These excellent but limited measurable outcomes are not due to examinations becoming easier, but rather to the industry and skills of teachers across the country, whom we salute.

What we demonstrate in these vivid accounts are the challenges, joys, and excitement of a truly creative learning community, where our preferred markers included extremely high staying-on rates post-16, with students and staff having remarkably high morale. As a community we arrived together at our credo *Learning Together, Achieving Together,* because together we had the brainpower, reflection, and imagination that far exceeded that of any solitary individual. We profoundly believed that every child and every adult has huge potential and good within them that only needs to be unlocked. The abilities of everyone should never be underestimated. We built with praise and recognition, encouragement rather than punishment, for everyone within our community. Joy, fun, and doing things with others underpinned everything.

We never stood still and never arrived, but our quests were for more effective and sustainable learning. We loved innovation and creativity and had the courage and support to take on new challenges. We did not always succeed, but we felt confident that we could learn from any failures and always improve on our previous best. We were avid readers and constant researchers, and valued and used 'failures' – things not always working out as we might have hoped or expected. We welcomed partnerships both within and outside the school. Colleagues and students were always encouraged to link and contribute outside the school as well as within it. We also enjoyed competition and challenge. We believed in a coherent, holistic curriculum where every part contributed to developing us all as lifelong learners. The creative arts and physical education were valued as much as literacy and numeracy, because without the support of a broad, coherent curriculum, many will never become both literate and numerate.

I was at Hampstead for 16 years, and it was only in my last years there that I could describe our school community in these terms. There is no such thing as a quick fix, and the early years had many challenges. I was lucky enough to be able – with others – to build a team of colleagues who shared my beliefs and aspirations, and it was only then that we were able to create the structures, bring in the partners, and take the calculated risks necessary for a creative learning community. Even so, as you will have read, we were not always successful. We missed opportunities and never did the very best for all our students. However, what these accounts do show is that – in the longer term – the majority of our community, both students and staff, are now making or continuing to make significant contributions towards a good society.

From my perspective as head I had a very simple focus: fun, valuing everyone, giving others (including students) supported opportunities, and the importance of modelling learning, hence my 'lead learners'. I also never accepted the prescribed curriculum, as Andrea Smith, Deirdre Broadbent, Olly Button, and Phil Taylor have said. I felt the curriculum and the environment for learning must be continuously reassessed to meet the current needs of the students as well as the needs of the community and wider society. Curricula devised on cigarette packets were never going to be suitable. I was involved with Valerie Bayliss in introducing the RSA skills-focused curriculum, and had I stayed at Hampstead for another year, we were scheduled to have been involved with that.

Equality in education through the majority of children attending local non-selective schools will always have to be fought for. In *The Spirit Level* Richard Wilkinson and Kate Pickett (2009) produce a vast body of evidence drawn from impeccable sources to show that everyone has a lower quality of life on all the important indicators, including education, health, well-being, and mortality rate, when they live in unequal societies. The greater the inequality, the poorer the quality of life for *all,* including the rich and privileged.

As can be seen from our powerful voices, it makes a great difference when young people are educated together in a non-selective comprehensive school, be it local education authority, voluntary-aided, or academy. When children experience playing a valued role within their non-selective community school, their friendships, tolerance, and aspirations enhance every aspect of their lives and raise their quality of life. This works towards far greater equality overall.

A good education, where all students are valued and can achieve, is the only way to develop the creative workforce we urgently need today. We will never overcome the major challenges we face locally, nationally, and globally unless the whole population contributes towards a better society. We will never achieve this if over 80 per cent of our young people experience continuous failures through selection, a narrow, out-of-date curriculum, and valueless testing. Increasing a hierarchy of unequal educational provision will ensure a culture of failure and a society with yet starker contrasts between the haves and the have-nots. This will totally destabilize our society.

In Hampstead School and all other successful comprehensive, non-selective schools with balanced intakes across the country, we have shown that we can provide the good, creative, and dynamic education where geese become swans.

We believe in Konoke Matsushita's statement: 'The core of management is the art of mobilizing and putting together the intellectual resources of all employees in the service of the firm' (Clarke, 1995: 240). This was our approach and should be the core purpose of all schools: mobilizing the intellectual resources of all students, staff, parents, and local communities, and putting them together to ensure the highest achievement for all. We are proud of high morale for all and would deem we had failed had there been low morale. At the time of writing, a poll of teachers suggests that over 55 per cent have low or very low morale (NUT, 2013). We take note of G.K. Chesterton's prophetic poem *The Secret People,* which could be said to describe the plight of education today:

> They have given us into the hands of new unhappy lords,
> Lords without anger or honour, who dare not carry their swords.
> They fight by shuffling papers; they have bright dead alien eyes;
> They look at our labour and laughter as a tired man looks at flies.
> And the load of their loveless pity is worse than the ancient wrongs,
> Their doors are shut in the evening; and they know no songs.
>
> (Chesterton, 1907)

This poem was written in the early twentieth century. S.J.M. Trenaman writing in the 1960s on adults' attitudes to education, before the majority of comprehensive schools were introduced, put it this way:

> The picture presented by this study is unquestionably that of an educationally stratified society. Like is attracted to like; those who have, seek for more. Educationally speaking, the population appears to be a hierarchy, pyramidal in distribution of attitudes and participation, rich and complex at the top, impoverished at the bottom.
>
> (Trenaman, 1967: 191)

We were moving to improve this during the late 1980s and 1990s, as the success of our more than 50 contributors to this book confirms. The massive attacks that have been mounted from Thatcher onwards, upon educationalists in general but most particularly on comprehensive non-selective education, will only speed up our return to such a highly unequal educational experience. This will deny the majority of children the joys and fun of learning that we have shown leads young people to become lifelong, creative learners.

Melissa Benn, in her book *School Wars,* argues powerfully for a national education service, held in the same high regard as our National Health Service used to be. She advocates:

> A service that allows the poorest family to feel confident that their child will receive a broadly similar educational start in life to their better-off peers, and one that promises to enrich and challenge all. A service based on neighbourhood schools – housed in well-designed, well-equipped, aesthetically pleasing and properly maintained buildings, enjoying plenty of outdoor space – with balanced intakes and a broad rich curriculum that will allow each child, whatever their talents, temperament or interests to flourish.
>
> (Benn, 2011: 201)

Most importantly she says:

> Rather than making schools compete for the easiest to teach or highest attaining pupils, local collaboration between schools on the crucial question of admissions – overseen by an impartial body, concerned above all with fairness – should ensure that each school has its share of both the most motivated and the hardest to teach. Without this we will surely continue with the situation we have now, where certain schools offload problems of the wider

society, and many of the country's poorest children are educated in
a tranche of poorly performing and poorly regarded schools.

(ibid.: 202)

Such a balanced intake was ours, even when our local private, voluntary-aided, and church schools were (and still are) selecting their intakes, both overtly and covertly, for music and other specialisms in order to raise their higher-achieving intake above – and to the disadvantage of – other surrounding schools. We were lucky that our confidence and enthusiasm made us a popular school. As far as was possible within the maintained sector, our intake was fairly administered by both the ILEA and later the Camden LEA. Now, successive governments have deliberately eroded this vital mechanism for educational equality. Memories are short, but those who to this day bear the deep scars of 11+ failure still smart as they tell of the impact of that early rejection. Can we afford such inequality? Would it not be far better to learn from the experiences of our contributors and respect the vast majority of our non-selective comprehensive schools that are still delivering success and are truly valued, as ours is, by students, teachers, parents, and their communities?

References

Balarin, M. and Lauder, H. (2009) 'The governance and administration of English primary education'. In R.J. Alexander, C. Doddington, J. Gray, L. Hargreaves, and R. Kershner (eds) *The Cambridge Primary Review Research Surveys*. Abingdon: Routledge.

Ball, S. (1990) *Politics and Policy Making in Education*. London: Routledge.

Benn, M. (2011) *School Wars: The battle for Britain's education*. London and New York: Verso.

Broadbent, D. (2008) 'Improving the grades of struggling GCSE pupils' listening tests'. *Classroom Music*, Autumn.

— (2009a) 'Composition'. *Classroom Music*, Spring.

— (2009b) 'Performing'. *Classroom Music*, Summer.

Chesterton, G.K. (1907) *The Secret People*. Online. www.theotherpages.org/poems/chester2.html#17 (accessed 23 January 2013).

Clarke, J. (1995) *Managing Innovation and Change*. London: Sage Publishing.

Demie, F., Lewis, K., and McLean, C. (2008) *Raising Achievement of Somali Pupils: Good practice in London schools*. London: Lambeth Research and Statistics Unit.

Department of Education and Science and the Welsh Office (1988) *Report of the National Curriculum Task Group on Assessment and Testing, Paul Black, Chair*. Online. www.educationengland.org.uk/documents/pdfs/1988-TGAT-report.pdf (accessed 23 January 2013).

Department for Education and Skills (2001) *Evaluation of the Effectiveness of the Statutory Arrangements for Newly Qualified Teachers*. Online. www.education.gov.uk/publications/eOrderingDownload/RR338.pdf (accessed 23 January 2013).

— (2007) *New arrivals excellence programme*. DVD. London: DfES. Ref:00426-2007 DVD-EN.

Dewey, J. (1916) *Democracy and Education*. New York: Free Press.

Earley, P. and Kinder, K. (1994) *Initiation Rites*. Slough: National Foundation for Educational Research.

Earley, P. and Weindling, D. (2004) *Understanding School Leadership*. London: Sage, Paul Chapman Publishing.

Erikson, E. (1980) *Identity and the Life Cycle: Selected papers*. New York and London: W.W. Norton & Company Inc.

Galton, M. and Macbeath, J. (2008) *Teachers Under Pressure*. London: Sage.

Gillard, D. (2011) *Education in England: A brief history*. Online. www.educationengland.org.uk/history (accessed 7 March 2013).

Ginnis, P. (2001) *The Teacher's Toolkit: Raise classroom achievement with strategies for every learner*. Carmarthen: Crown House.

Grant, M. (2012) *Comment as Link Inspector for Hampstead School 1990–6: Camden LEA*. Unpublished correspondence (Peter Mitchell).

Heilbronn, R. and Jones, C. (1997) *New Teachers in an Urban Comprehensive*. Staffs: Trentham Books.

Imison, T. and Taylor, P. (2001) *Managing ICT in the Secondary School*. Oxford: Heinemann.

Leithwood, K. and Riehl, C. (2003) *What We Know About Successful School Leadership*. Nottingham: National College for School Leadership.

MacBeath J., Kirwan, T., and Myers, K. (2001) *The Impact of Study Support: A study into the effects of participation in out-of-school-hours learning on the academic attainment, attitudes and attendance of secondary school students.* London: DfES.

Macpherson, W. (1999) *The Stephen Lawrence Inquiry.* Online. www.archive. official-documents.co.uk/document/cm42/4262/4262.htm (accessed 23 January 2013).

Mortimore, P. (2008) 'In Memoriam'. *Guardian Education*, 3 June 2008. Online. www.guardian.co.uk/education/2008/jun/03/schools.uk1 (accessed 23 January 2013).

National Advisory Committee on Creative and Cultural Education (1999) *All Our Futures: Creativity and culture in education.* Online. http://sirkenrobinson.com/skr/pdf/allourfutures.pdf (accessed 23 January 2013).

National Union of Teachers (2013) *A Verdict on the Coalition Government's Education Policy: A survey of the teaching profession.* January 2013. Online. www.teachers.org.uk/files/NUT%20analysis.doc (accessed 7 July 2013).

Rasmussen, J. (2011) 'Education for Somali students in London: Challenges and strategies'. *Macalester Abroad: Research and writing from off-campus study,* 3.1 (2011): 4.

Rayner, L. (1999) 'Weighing a century with a website: Teaching Year 9 to be critical'. *Teaching History,* 96, 13–21.

Savage, G. (1947) *Speech to Head teachers on the London School Plan* (unpublished personal papers, Peter Newsam).

Stoll, L., Bolam, R., McMahon, A., Wallace, M., and Thomas, S. (2006) 'Professional learning communities: A review of the literature'. *Journal of Educational Change,* 7 (4), 221–58.

Strang, J., Masterson, P., and Button, O. (2006) *Attitudes, Skills and Knowledge: How to teach learning to learn in the secondary school.* Carmarthen: Crown House.

Sullivan, J. (2000) 'Stand and deliver – The teacher's integrity?'. In C. Watkins, C. Lodge and R. Best (eds), *Tomorrow's Schools – Towards Integrity.* London: Routledge.

Taylor, P. (1997) 'IT: Every teacher's second subject?'. In R. Heilbronn and C. Jones (eds), *New Teachers in an Urban Comprehensive School.* Staffs: Trentham.

Tilbrook, G. (2012) *Comment as Head of the Education Development Centre, 1990–2011.* Camden LEA. Unpublished correspondence, Peter Mitchell.

Trenaman, S.J.M. (1967) *Communication and Comprehension.* London: Longmans.

Watkins, C. (2003) *Learning: A sense-maker's guide.* London: Association of Teachers and Lecturers.

— (2005) *Classrooms as Learning Communities: What's in it for schools?* London: Falmer Routledge.

— (2010) *Learning, Performance and Improvement.* Research Matters series, No 34. London: IOE, International Network for School Improvement.

Watkins, C., Carnell, E., and Lodge, C. (2007) *Effective Learning in Classrooms.* London: Sage.

Wilkinson, R. and Pickett, K. (2009) *The Spirit Level*. London: Allen Lane.

Young, M. (2009) 'What are schools for?'. In H. Lauder, J. Porter, and H. Daniels (eds), *Critical Perspectives on Education*. London: Routledge.

Index